Project Evaluation and Discounted Cash Flow

A Reassessment and an Alternative Suggestion

PROJECT EVALUATION AND DISCOUNTED CASH FLOW

A Reassessment and an Alternative Suggestion

by

H. P. J. HEUKENSFELDT JANSEN

1977

NORTH-HOLLAND PUBLISHING COMPANY
AMSTERDAM · NEW YORK · OXFORD

© NORTH-HOLLAND PUBLISHING COMPANY – 1977

ISBN North-Holland for this volume: 07204 0480 0

Publishers:

NORTH-HOLLAND PUBLISHING COMPANY
AMSTERDAM · NEW YORK · OXFORD

Sole distributors for the U.S.A. and Canada:

ELSEVIER NORTH-HOLLAND, INC.
52 VANDERBILT AVENUE
NEW YORK, N.Y. 10017

Library of Congress Cataloging in Publication Data

Heukensfeldt Jansen, Henricus Philippus Jacobus.
Project evaluation and discounted cash flow.

Bibliography: p. 197
Includes index.

1. Capital investments.   2. Cash flow.
I. Title.   II. Title: Discounted cash flow.

HG4028.C4H48   658.1'52   76-16803

PRINTED IN THE NETHERLANDS

ACKNOWLEDGEMENTS

I am deeply indebted to the Royal Dutch Group of companies with which I served for 25 years, for the specialised knowledge which has enabled me to write this book. It contains many examples from actual experience but the views expressed and the conclusions drawn are mine and not necessarily those of Shell.

Mr. D.P. Wade very kindly read an early version of the manuscript. Thanks to his helpful comments the book gained much in clarity and exposition. I owe him a great debt.

I am also much indebted to many former colleagues with whom I have had stimulating discussions over a long period. In particular I should mention Mr. J. van Embden on whose analysis of the problems of growth I have heavily drawn. Also I should mention Messrs. J.H. Austin, P.M. Inman, D.J. Watson, P.W.R.C. Beck, J.J. de Kort and S.J.Q. Robinson. If there are others whose names I have not mentioned I hope they will accept my thanks and apologies. They equally belong to those to whom I wish to express my gratitude.

However the responsibility for the views expressed is entirely mine. Direct contributions are acknowledged in the text.

I am very grateful to the publishers for the care they have taken in the production of this book, and for the help they have given me. I am sure that the book would not have been produced without the kind assistance of their economics editor Miss E.M. van Koten and their desk editor Miss A. Gothmann.

Last but not least I wish to express my gratitude to those who typed the various versions of the manuscript for me. Mrs. June Orr, Mrs. L. Thornton and Mrs. M. Dekker. Apart from text, I presented them with formulas and tables which cannot have been easy to type. They did the work cheerfully and with great diligence and skill. I owe them an immense debt.

CONTENTS

INTRODUCTION

It has become customary in recent years for the attractiveness of a new investment to be assessed by using the technique of the Discounted Cash Flow. This practice has become so generally accepted that the whole procedure of projecting the profitability of a new investment into future years by financial estimates (as opposed to the criterion itself for assessing the attractiveness of the cash flow of the new investment) is often referred to as the DCF technique. This study deals with the criterion only.

On the face of it, the widespread adoption of the technique is surprising because the success of the business in the market is normally measured not in terms of discounted cash flow but in terms of very different criteria such as net income, and net income as a percentage of net capital employed and/or the ability of the company to finance its own growth if funds are not available from the market, and/or the ability of the company to pay dividends on its shares etc. After all that is the information which is published by the company in its annual accounts, and that is the information which the Chairman of the company has to present to the shareholders. The annual accounts are of vital importance to the life of the company because they perform four closely related functions:

(1) They are of direct significance for the continuation of the business.

(2) They play a major role in the decisions of financiers as to whether they are prepared to invest money in the business (e.g., for expansion) and if so on what terms.

(3) They play a major role in the formulation of the objectives.

(4) Sound financial accounts are a sine qua non for a comfortable living of those who work in the company.

Since the DCF criterion reflects information which is not directly available in, and indeed divergent from that shown in the accounts, it is appropriate to analyse in detail whether in compensation for the apparent lack of logic which the DCF criterion displays, it has advantages to offer which justify its use.

This study attempts to make a contribution towards the analysis of the problem. In doing so it confines itself entirely to one aspect of project evaluation, i.e., the criterion for assessing the attractiveness of the investment, with particular reference to the nature and purpose of project evaluation. The significance of the criterion within the context of the growth of the business will also be analysed. Other aspects of project evaluation such as the assembly of the basic data will not be discussed. Nevertheless, the careful and intelligent assembly of the basic data is by far the most important part of the procedure. Basic data reflect judgement, and the planning manager of any company is the only judge of the problems which his company faces. Therefore a study which generalizes on project evaluation can only show how the basic data should be put in their place like soldiers on a parade ground. It can comment on the interrelationship of the figures, but it cannot comment on the quality of the basic data. It has therefore been assumed throughout this study, that the basic data are the most reliable ones available. However, the evaluator is well advised always to bear in mind the remark by Mr. Moroney that the English word 'fictitious' and the English word 'figure' derive from the same Latin source.* Thus project evaluation is an art and the technique is the tool with which that art is carried out. However valuable that tool, even if it were a hammer made of gold with precious stones inlaid, it will not prevent the evaluator from hitting his fingers if he does not use it with care and skill.

Details of the calculations are shown, so as to give the reader a clear insight into the structure of the models which have been used. The examples have been taken from or inspired by the chemical industry because that is where the experience of the author lies. However the principles can be 'translated' to apply to other industries,

*See M.J. Moroney, Facts from Figures, Penguin Books, edition 1967, page 56.

although the relative weight of the various factors which come into play may vary considerably between industries. Insofar as the models of this study apply to the chemical industry, it may be said that this book is a case study.

CHAPTER I

A STUDY MODEL – PROCEDURE AND DEFINITIONS

In Tables 1.1 and 1.2 details are given of the calculation of the cash flow, earning power, present day value, net income and net capital employed of a project 'P'.

The various items which make up the calculation are discussed in the same sequence in which they are shown in the tables. The numbers against the items correspond with the lines shown in the tables.

Units
– Physical quantities in units of 'tons'.
– Financial quantities in units of 'financial units', abbreviated FU's. It is assumed that FU's have a stable value, i.e., there is no inflation.
– Time quantities in units of 'years', except where otherwise stated.
– Figures shown between brackets ( ) are negative figures.

(1) *Sales*
Sales quantities in thousands of tons.

(2) *Increases in Sales,* (3) *Debtors and* (4) *Stocks*
Increases in sales, debtors and stocks in thousands of tons as compared with the previous year.

(5) *Netback*
Net proceeds at plant, after deducting all sales expenses, commissions, sales margins, transport costs duties, turnover taxes, etc. It is assumed that all sales are made ex plant.

H.P.J. Heukensfeldt Jansen

TABLE 1.1

Calculation of the cash flow for project 'P' (lines 1–4 in tons, lines 5–20 in FU's)
for years 1–6.

	1	2	3	4	5	6
(1) Sales			156.0	162.2	168.7	175.5
(2) Increase in sales			156.0	6.2	6.5	6.8
(3) Debtors (2 months)			26.0	1.0	1.1	1.1
(4) Stocks (1 month)			13.0	0.5	0.6	0.5
(5) Netback @ FU 28/ton			4368.0	4541.6	4723.6	4914.0
(6) Variable costs for sales @ FU 12/t0n			(1872.0)	(1946.4)	(2024.4)	(2106.0)
(7) Variable costs for stocks @ FU 12/ton			(156.0)	(6.0)	(7.2)	(6.0)
(8) Margin			2340.0	2589.2	2692.0	2802.0
(9) Fixed costs			(816.2)	(816.2)	(816.2)	(816.2)
(10) Pre-operational expenses		(89.5)	(134.3)			
(11) Cash before tax		(89.5)	1389.5	1773.0	1875.8	1985.8
(12) Stock valuation @ FU 20.445/ton[b]			265.8	10.2	12.3	10.2
(13) Depreciation 10%			(746.1)	(746.1)	(746.1)	(746.1)
(14) Taxable		(89.5)	909.2	1037.1	1142.0	1249.9
(15) Tax (50%)		44.8	(454.6)	(518.6)	(571.0)	(625.0)
(16) Cash generation (11)–(15)		(44.7)	934.9	1254.4	1304.8	1360.8
(17) Capital expenditure	(2984.4)	(2984.4)	(1492.2)			
(18) Debtors			(728.0)	(28.0)	(30.8)	(30.8)
(19) Other working capital			(339.2)			
(20) Cash flow	(2984.4)	(3029.1)	(1624.5)	1226.4	1274.0	1330.0

[a]Values p.a. for years 13 to 22.
[b]Cost of production at full capacity including 10% depreciation (in FU/ton).

Variable costs	12.000
Fixed costs (816.2/185)	4.412
Depreciation (746.1/185)	4.033
Total	20.445

TABLE 1.1 (continued)
Calculation of the cash flow for project 'P' (lines 1–4 in tons, lines 5–20 in FU's)
for years 7–22 and the total.

7	8	9	10	11	12	13–22[a]	Total[c]
182.5	185.0	185.0	185.0	185.0	185.0	185.0	
0.7	2.5						
1.2	0.4						30.8
0.6	0.2						15.4
5110.0	5180.0	5180.0	5180.0	5180.0	5180.0	5180.0	
(2190.0)	(2220.0)	(2220.0)	(2220.0)	(2220.0)	(2220.0)	(2220.0)	
(7.2)	(2.4)						(184.8)
2912.8	2957.6	2960.0	2960.0	2960.0	2960.0	2960.0	
(816.2)	(816.2)	(816.2)	(816.2)	(816.2)	(816.2)	(816.2)	
2096.6	2141.4	2143.8	2143.8	2143.8	2143.8	2143.8	41185.8
12.3	4.1						314.9
(746.1)	(746.1)	(746.1)	(746.1)	(746.1)	(746.1)		(7461.0)
1362.8	1399.4	1397.7	1397.7	1397.7	1397.7	2143.8	
(681.4)	(699.7)	(698.9)	(698.9)	(698.9)	(698.9)	(1071.9)	(17020.1)
1415.2	1441.7	1444.9	1444.9	1444.9	1444.9	1071.9	24165.7
							(7461.0)
(33.6)	(11.2)						(862.4)
							(339.2)
1381.6	1430.5	1444.9	1444.9	1444.9	1444.9	1071.9	15503.1

[c]Residual value and total cash flow.		Cash flow (years 1–22)	15503.1
Stocks	314.9	Residual value	1516.5
Debtors	862.4		
Other working capital	339.2	Total	17019.6
Total	1516.5		

H.P.J. Heukensfeldt Jansen

TABLE 1.2

Calculation of earning power, present day value, net income and net capital employed for project 'P' (lines 20–36 and 38–40 in FU's, line 37 in %) for years 1–6.

	1	2	3	4	5	6
(20) Cash flow	(2984-4)	(3029.1)	(1624.5)	1226.4	1274.0	1330.0
(21) Factor 13%[b]	0.885	0.783	0.693	0.613	0.543	0.480
(22) Factor 14%[b]	0.877	0.769	0.675	0.592	0.519	0.456
(23) Factor 8%[b]	0.926	0.857	0.794	0.735	0.681	0.630
(24) Cash before tax		(89.5)	1389.5	1773.0	1875.8	1985.8
(25) Depreciation			(746 .1)	(746 .1)	(746 .1)	(746 .1)
(26) Stock valuation			265.8	10.2	12.3	10.2
(27) Tax 50%		44.8	454.6)	(518.6)	(571.0)	(625.0)
(28) Net income		(44.7)	454.6	518.5	571.0	624.9
(29) Capital expenditure at cost	2984.4	5968.8	7461.0	7461.0	7461.0	7461.0
(30) Depreciation (cum.)			(746.1)	(1492.2)	(2238.3)	(2984.4)
(31) Book value	2984.4	5968.8	6714.9	5968.8	5222.7	4476.6
(32) Stock valuation			265.8	276.0	288.3	298.5
(33) Debtors			728.0	756.0	786.8	817.6
(34) Other working capital			339.2	339.2	339.2	339.2
(35) Losses		44.7				
(36) Net capital employed	2984.4	6013.5	8047.9	7340.0	6637.0	5931.9
(37) NI/NCE	0	(0.1)	5.6	7.1	8.6	10.5
(38) Net income (cum.) minus:			409.9	928.4	1499.4	2124.3
(39) Cash flow (cum.)	(2984.4)	(6013.5)	(7638.0)	(6411.6)	(5137.6)	(3807.6)
(40) Net capital employed	2984.4	6013.5	8047.9	7340.0	6637.0	5913.9

[a]Values p.a. for years 13 to 22, except for lines 21–23 which present the sum total of the factors for these years.

TABLE 1.2 (continued)

Calculation of earning power, present day value, net income and net capital employed for project 'P' (lines 20–36 and 38–40 in FU's, line 37 in %) for years 7–22 and the total.

7	8	9	10	11	12	13–22[a]	Total
1381.6	1430.5	1444.9	1444.9	1444.9	1444.9	1071.9	17019.6[c]
0.425	0.376	0.333	0.295	0.261	0.231	1.253	
0.400	0.351	0.308	0.270	0.237	0.208	1.084	
					Earning power:	$13 + \dfrac{120.6}{401.0} = 13.3\%$	
0.583	0.540	0.500	0.463	0.429	0.397	2.665	
2096.6	2141.4	2143.8	2143.8	2143.8	2143.8	2143.8	41185.8
(746.1)	(746.1)	(746.1)	(746.1)	(746.1)	(746.1)		(7461.0)
12.3	4.1						314.9
(681.4)	(699.7)	(698.9)	(698.9)	(698.9)	(698.9)	1071.9	17020.1
681.4	699.7	698.8	698.8	698.8	698.8	1071.9	17019.6
7461.0	7461.0	7461.0	7461.0	7461.0	7461.0		
(3730.5)	(4476.6)	(5222.7)	(5968.8)	(6714.9)	(7461.0)	(7461.0)	
3730.5	2984.4	2238.3	1492.2	746.1	0	0	
310.8	314.9	314.9	314.9	314.9	314.9	314.9	
851.2	862.4	862.4	862.4	862.4	862.4	862.4	
339.2	339.2	339.2	339.2	339.2	339.2	339.2	
5231.7	4500.9	3754.8	3008.7	2262.6	1516.5	1516.5	
13.0	15.5	18.6	23.2	30.9	46.1	70.7	
2805.7	3505.4	4204.2	4903.0	5601.8	6300.6	7372.5	etc.
(2426.0)	(995.5)	449.4	1894.3	3339.2	4784.1	5856.0	etc.
5231.7	4500.9	3754.8	3008.7	2262.6	1516.5	1516.5	

[b]Present day value: 13%–120.6, 14%–(180.4), 8%–3234.8.
[c]Including Residual value.

(6) *Variable Costs for Sales and* (7) *for Stocks*

All manufacturing costs which are proportionate to product output such as costs of electricity, raw materials, steam, packing materials, etc. Variable costs are incurred in respect of manufacture for sales and manufacture for stocks.

(8) *Margin*

This is defined as the difference between netback and variable costs.

(9) *Fixed Costs*

Fixed costs are all costs which are not proportionate to product output, i.e., operating labour (including social charges), maintenance costs and general overheads such as salaries, administrative costs, transport costs, insurance, etc.

(10) *Pre-operational Expenses*

Pre-operational expenses are costs which are incurred for bringing the new plant and equipment into operation, e.g., additional overheads, training of staff, over-consumption of raw materials, etc.

(11) *Cash Before Tax*

'Cash before tax' is defined as:

$$\begin{array}{ll} & \text{Netback} \\ \text{Minus:} & \text{Variable costs} \\ \text{Minus:} & \text{Fixed costs} \\ \text{Minus:} & \text{Pre-operational expenses} \end{array}$$

(12) *Stock Valuation*

For fiscal purposes stocks are valued at cost at full capacity including 10% depreciation. Thus the stock valuation per ton is equal to:

Variable costs per ton

Plus: $$\frac{\text{Fixed costs}}{\text{Annual capacity}}$$

Plus: $$\frac{0.1 \times \text{Capital expenditure}}{\text{Annual capacity}}$$

See footnote b to Table 1.1.

This valuation does not take into account the build-up of output to full capacity, but the simplification, which has been made for the sake of convenience, is of little importance to the principles analysed in this study.

(13) *Fiscal Depreciation*
Fiscal depreciation is assumed to be 10%, and equal to the commercial depreciation. See also under (25).

(14) *Taxable income*
Taxable income is equal to:

Cash before tax

Plus: Stock valuation

Minus: Fiscal depreciation

The stock valuation has been added back because 'cash before tax' has been obtained after deducting variable costs for stocks and full fixed costs. Taxable income should of course be computed after deducting only that portion of variable and fixed costs which applies to quantities sold.

(15) *Tax*
The new investment is assumed to be part of an existing complex. Therefore as a result of the new investment incurring a loss in year 2 due to pre-operational expenses, there is a corresponding reduction of taxable income for the complex as a whole. The project has therefore been credited with a negative tax, i.e., a tax credit in year 2.

(16) *Cash Generation*
    Cash generation is equal to:

Cash before tax
Minus: Tax

or to:

Net income
Plus: Depreciation
Minus: Increases in stock valuation
See also under (28).

The term 'cash flow' is frequently used in publications for what has been called here 'cash generation'. In this study this term will be reserved entirely to indicate an actual flow of 'cash', i.e., it is cash generation minus outlay for fixed investment, land and working capital. See also under (20).

(17) *Capital Expenditure*
    Expenditure on plant and equipment which in this case is spread over three years. The last payments are made in the year in which the plant commences commercial production.

(18) *Debtors*
    Increases in debtors each year, i.e., the physical quantities shown under (3) multiplied by unit netback of £ 28/ton.

(19) *Increases in Other Working Capital*
    Increases in stocks of maintenance materials *plus* minimum cash to operate the new investment.
    It has been assumed in this example that stocks of raw materials bought in from third parties are equal to creditors, i.e., stocks are financed by creditors.

(20) *Cash Flow*
    The cash flow is equal to:

        Cash generation
Minus: Capital expenditure
Minus: Increases in debtors
Minus: Increases in other working capital
Plus: Residual value in the year after the last operational year.

See also under (16).

Residual Value
The residual value is equal to:
        Stock valuation
Plus: Debtors
Plus: Other working capital

See also footnote c to Table 1.1.

(21) *Discount Factors*
The formula which has been used for the discount factors is:

$$F_n = \frac{1}{(1 + R)^n} \quad \text{(for year } n\text{)},$$

where R is the rate of discount expressed as a fraction.

Any refinements in the factor, e.g., to take account of the fact that the cash flow comes in as a stream during the course of the year, and not, as has been assumed in the formula, as a lump sum at the end of the year, have been ignored because the difference is well within the margin of error.

The factor for residual value is the factor for year 23.

(22) *Earning Power*
This will be abbreviated as EP.

(23) *Present Day Value*
This will be abbreviated as PDV.

(24) *Cash Before Tax*
Identical to (11).

(25) *Depreciation*
Book depreciation which in this case is identical to fiscal depreciation. See under (13).

(26) *Stock Valuation*
Identical to (12).

(27) *Tax*
Identical to (15).

(28) *Net Income*
Net income is equal to:

	Cash before tax
Minus:	Depreciation
Plus:	Stock valuation
Minus:	Tax

(29) *Capital Expenditure at Cost*
Capital expenditure as under (17) shown cumulatively.

(30) *Depreciation (cum.)*
Depreciation as under (25) shown cumulatively.

(31) *Book Value*
Cumulative capital expenditure minus cumulative depreciation, i.e., (29) minus (30).

(32) *Stock Valuation*
Stock Valuation as under (26) shown cumulatively.

(33) *Debtors*
Debtors as under (18) shown cumulatively.

(34) *Other Working Capital*
Other working capital as under (19) shown cumulatively.

(35) *Losses*
Losses as under (28) shown cumulatively until cumulatively net income becomes positive.

(36) *Net Capital Employed*
This is equal to:

> Book value
Plus: Stock valuation
Plus: Debtors
Plus: Other working capital
Plus: Cumulative losses

(37) *Net Income / Net Capital Employed*
The ratio of net income to net capital employed in %, i.e., $(28) \div (36) \times 100$. It will be abbreviated as NI/NCE.

Financial Accounts Profitability Criteria
Net income, net capital employed and net income / net capital employed.

(38) (39) (40) *Net Income (cum.), Cash Flow (cum.), Net Capital Employed*
The net capital employed is equal to the cumulative net income minus the cumulative cash flow, provided the cumulative net income is positive. If it is not, then the (negative) cumulative net income should be treated as being equal to 0.[1]

---

[1] I owe this relationship to Mr. J.J. de Kort.

CHAPTER 2

THE PRINCIPLES OF EARNING POWER AND PRESENT DAY VALUE

The first task is to review the nature of the two criteria of the discounted cash flow, i.e., earning power (EP) and present day value (PDV). It will be seen that each criterion can be interpreted in two different ways.

The *earning power* of a cash flow is defined as the discount rate at which the aggregate present day value of that cash flow is equal to 0. The meaning of this can be explained in the following terms.

If an amount of FU 300 is invested at the present time and the interest rate is 5%, then the value of that investment (including interest) after two years is:

$$FU\ 300 \times (1.05)^2,$$

i.e., FU 300 at compound interest of 5%. Or, reversing this calculation, if a comparison is made between the value in year 0 of:

(1)   a sum of FU 300 in year 0, and
(2)   a sum of FU 300 in year 2,

then the following would result:

(1)   value in year 0 of FU 300 in year 0: FU 300, and
(2)   value in year 0 of FU 300 in year 2: $FU\ 300 / (1.05)^2 = FU\ 272$.

Thus the present day value of FU 300 in year 2 is FU 272. It would make no difference to an investor whether he receives FU 300 in year 2 or FU 272 in year 0 'at the present time'.

H.P.J. Heukensfeldt Jansen

The present day value (PDV) of a cash flow is the aggregate of the present day values of each of the annual cash flows. The earning power is defined as the discount rate at which the aggregate (or the sum total) of the present day values of each of the cash flows in future years is equal to zero. Thus the earning power of project 2.1 shown in Table 2.1 over a life time of 4 years, is 20%.

TABLE 2.1

The calculation of the earning power of project 2.1 (in FU's). The life time of project 2.1 is 4 years.

Year	Cash flow of project 2.1 (1)	Discount factor 20% (2)	Discounted cash flow (3)
1	(300)	1.000	(300)
2	170	0.833	142
3	140	0.694	97
4	105	0.579	61
	Present day value of the aggregate cash flow		0

The principle of earning power can be interpreted in two different ways:

(1)   the reducing balance interpretation, and
(2)   the compound interest interpretation.

The reducing balance interpretation is illustrated in Table 2.2.

The interest in year 2 on the investment of FU 300 outstanding at the end of year 1, is 20% of FU 300 = FU 60 (column 2). In year 2 the total cash flow is FU 170. Therefore an amount of FU 170 minus FU 60 equals FU 110 (column 3) is available for paying out the original investment of FU 300 leaving at the end of year 2 an investment of FU 190 outstanding (column 4). The interest in year 3 on the outstanding investment is 20% of FU 190 = FU 38 (column 2). The cash flow in year 3 is FU 140 which leaves an amount of FU 140 − FU 38 = FU 102 for paying out the investment (column 3). The investment outstanding at the end of year 3 is therefore FU

TABLE 2.2

The reducing balance interpretation of earning power for project 2.1 (in FU's). The life time of project 2.1 is 4 years. A breakdown of the cash flow (column 1) into sums available for pay-out of the investment (column 3) and interest 20% (column 2) on the non-paid-out investment (column 4). Column (1) = column (2) + column (3). Column (4) in year $n + 1$ = column (4) in year n minus Column (3) in year $n + 1$.

Year	Cash flow (1)	Interest 20% (2)	To pay-out investment (3)	Balance investment (4)
1	(300)			300
2	170	60	110	190
3	140	38	102	88
4	105	17	88	0
Total	115	115	300	

$190 - FU\,102 = FU\,88$ (column 4). The interest in year 4 on the outstanding investment of FU 88 is 20% of FU 88 = FU 17 (column 2). The cash flow in year 4 is FU 105 leaving an amount of FU $105 - FU\,17 = FU\,88$ (column 3), to pay out the investment. This is exactly equal to the investment of FU 88 outstanding at the end of year 3.

The table shows that:

(a)   the investment of FU 300 has been completely repaid at the end of year 4, and

(b)   the cash flow has, apart from paying out the investment, generated sufficient means to yield a return of 20% each year on that part of the investment which has not been paid out.

Point (b) may also be illustrated as in Table 2.3.

The discounting technique thus makes it possible for the cash flow each year to be divided into an investment repayment component on the one hand, and a return on the outstanding investment on the other hand. This return which is constant during the life time of the project applies to a declining investment. It is called earning power, and is calculated by selecting a discount factor which results in a zero aggregate present day value for the cash flow. Clearly earning power can only be calculated if the cash flow in one or more years is negative

TABLE 2.3

The split up of the cash flow into a component for replacement of the investment and a component to pay interest on the outstanding investment for project 2.1 (in FU's).

End of year	Outstanding balances (1)	Interest 20% on (1) (2)
1	88 + 102 + 110 = 300	17 + 21 + 22 = 60
2	88 + 102 = 190	17 + 21 = 38
3	88 = 88	17 = 17
	264 + 204 + 110 = 578	51 + 42 + 22 = 115

because otherwise a zero present day value for the aggregate cash flow would not result. Therefore there must be an investment for earning power to be calculated. It would not be possible to express the profitability of a straight trade transaction in terms of earning power because in such cases there is no investment (assuming that there are no stocks or debtors).

The analysis has shown that the return does not include in any way interest accruing from investment of the cash flows. It is a remuneration at simple interest. For example in the cash flow previously analysed the return on the investment which has been outstanding for 3 years, i.e., FU 88 is:

3 times 20% of FU 88 = FU 51,

whilst at compound interest it would have been:

FU's

Interest on cash flow accruing in year 1:	$17 \times (1.2)^2 =$	24
2:	17×1.2 =	20
3:	17×1 =	17
Total		61

However an alternative interpretation of earning power which presupposes compound interest on the cash flow and on the investment, is also possible – the compound interest interpretation. Using again the previous example it is represented in Table 2.4.

TABLE 2.4

The compound interest interpretation of earning power for project 2.1 (in FU's).

	Years				
	1	2	3	4	Total
Cash flow	(300)	170	140	105	115
Available funds					
Positive cash flow		170	140	105	415
20% interest on 170			34	34	68
20% interest on 140				28	28
20% interest on 20% interest of 170, i.e., 20% on 34				7	7
		170	174	174	518
Investment	300				300
20% interest on 300		60	60	60	180
20% interest on 20% of 300, i.e., 20% on 60			12	12	24
20% interest on 20% of 300 + 60				14	14
	300	60	72	86	518

This is a literal interpretation of the normal discounting formula for calculating the earning power because this formula:

$$-I + \frac{F_1}{1 + S} + \frac{F_2}{(1 + S)^2} + \frac{F_3}{(1 + S)^3} = 0, \tag{1}$$

where I is the investment; F_1, F_2, F_3 the cash flows in years 1, 2, 3;

and S the earning power (as a fraction), can be restated to read:

$$I(1 + S)^3 = F_1 (1 + S)^2 + F_2 (1 + S) + F_3.$$

In the case of the previous example:

$$300 \times (1.2)^3 = 170 \times (1.2)^2 + 140 \times 1.2 + 105 = 518.$$

Whereas the original formula (1) is backward-looking in the sense that it looks at the future value of the cash flow in present day terms, the restated formula (2) is forward-looking in the sense that it states what the position will be in future years if compound interest is earned on the cash flow. The formula shows that the cash flow increased by compound interest on it, is exactly equal to the investment plus compound interest on it, at the earning power rate of interest. In other words the investment can be paid out and compound interest on it is available provided the cash flow is increased by compound interest on it at the earning power rate of interest. It will be seen that this interpretaion – the compound interest interpretation – is very different from the reducing balance interpretation. The latter interpretation of earning power is by far the most practical.

Analysing the reducing balance interpretation further, it gives an indication how much interest on outstanding loans can be paid each year over the life time of the project. If as in the previous example an amount of FU 300 is invested, and this is financed by a loan of an equal amount, then interest of 20% can be paid on the loans outstanding each year. In other words earning power establishes how much 'room' there is available during the life time of the project for defraying the interest on any loans – the 'cost of capital'. This principle is one of the mainstays of the technique of the discounted cash flow. It can also be illustrated by specifying the details of the build-up of the cash flow of project 2.1 (see Table 2.5) and then working out the source and disposition of funds (see Table 2.6).

From Table 2.2 it can be seen that the available funds allow for a repayment of FU 110 in year 2, FU 102 in year 3 and FU 88 in year 4. The outstanding balances of the investment are correspondingly

TABLE 2.5
The components of the cash flow of project 2.1 (in FU's).

	Years			
	1	2	3	4
Cash generation	(250)	170	140	55
Debtors	(50)			50
Cash flow	(300)	170	140	105

Earning power: 20%

TABLE 2.6
The relationship between earning power and the cost of capital for project 2.1 (in FU's).

	Years			
	1	2	3	4
Source of funds				
Cash generation	(250)	170	140	55
Debtors	(50)			50
Loan (in)	300			
Total	0	170	140	105
Disposition of funds				
Interest 20% on outstanding loan (no taxes)[a]		60	38	17
Loan (out)		110	102	88
Total	0	170	140	105

[a]The interest of 20% is equal to the earning power of the cash flow.

reduced (see Table 2.2, column 4) and the non-paid-out investment is financed by the outstanding loans (see Table 2.7). The financial position is in balance if 20% interest is paid on the outstanding loans and this is equal to the earning power of the cash flow.

TABLE 2.7

The finance of the outstanding balances of the investment by loans and the resulting cost of capital for project 2.1 (in FU's).

	Years			
	1	2	3	4
Outstanding balances of the investment[a]	300	190	88	0
Outstanding loans	300	190	88	0
Interest 20% on outstanding loan		60	38	17

[a]See Table 2.2, column (4).

Thus earning power sets an upper limit to the rate of interest (the cost of capital) which the cash flow can carry. If earning power and the cost of capital are equal, then the cost of capital fits so to speak into the slot which earning power leaves it.

There are two further parameters besides interest, which have to fit into the slot, and which are facets of the cost of capital; the length of the loan and the redemption pattern. In the theory of the discounted cash flow the life time of the project and the length of the loan are implicitly assumed to be equal. Yet they are entirely unrelated parameters. The former reflects economic structure or technical factors which determine the period during which the project is expected to be economically viable, whilst the latter should reflect the period during which finance is required by, or is available to the company. These periods are only equal by a remote chance. Furthermore the redemption pattern of the loan is a resultant of the assumed life time, and also of the relationship between the negative cash flow (investment) and the positive cash flow which it generates, and this pattern is different for every project. In fact the redemption pattern (or its obverse, the outstanding investment each year) although expressed in financial terms, reflects economic structure in all its variety, whilst the cost of capital reflects market forces in the financial world. Thus by comparing loosely earning power with the cost of capital it is tacitly assumed that two very important facets of the cost of capital – the length of the loan and the redemption pattern – fit precisely into the slot which not the forces of the financial market, but economic structure provides for it. In many cases this may be true but seldom if ever is it scrutinized for its validity.

It follows that an earning power for a new investment without a specification of the corresponding life time of the project is completely meaningless, because the interest on any loan should also be related to the length of that loan. A cost of a loan of, e.g., 10% to be redeemed after 4 years is not the same as the cost of a loan of 10% if it is to be redeemed in 10 years. Table 2.8 gives a detailed example.

The cash flow of project 2.1 and project 2.2 both have an earning power of 20%. In case A the loan of FU 300 is repaid after 4 years whilst in case B it is repaid after 7 years. It is not surprising that the redemption pattern of the two loans is entirely different. Therefore they cannot be compared. Yet in the literature and also in the financial press, earning power is almost always given without a specification of the life time of the project, and thus the 'cost of capital' is not related to the duration of the loan (which is equal to that life time). Examples of this loose phrasing are statements such as: 'The minimum acceptable rate of return of the new investment should be 10% by the DCF method, because that is the cost of capital.' Or, 'The cut-off point is 12% return by the DCF method.'

There is a further reason why it is meaningless to quote an earning power without a corresponding life time; and that is because for a given investment the earning power is higher the longer is the assumed life time of the project. This is due to the fact that with a longer life time the positive cash flow is higher, leaving a larger sum of money to pay a return on the outstanding investment, after repayment of that investment. This is illustrated by comparing the cash flow of project 2.1 which has a life time of 4 years (see Table 2.1) with the cash flow of the same project on the assumption that it has a life time of 5 years

TABLE 2.8
The cost of capital and the lifetime of the project (in FU's).

	Case A	Case B
	Cash flow of project 2.1	Cash flow of project 2.2
Year 1	(300)	(300)
2	170	90
3	140	90
4	105	90
5		90
6		90
7		90
Earning power (%)	20	20

Details of the loan to finance the investment:

Interest (%)	20	20
Length of the loan (years)	4	7

Redemption pattern:

Year 2	110	30
3	102	36
4	88	44
5		52
6		63
7		75
Total	300	300

(project 2.3). The two cash flows are shown in Table 2.9. By an analysis similar to that of Table 2.2 (whereby the positive cash flow of project 2.1 is split into an amount available for pay-out of the investment and interest on the outstanding balances of that investment), the sums of money available to pay interest on the outstanding balances of the investment of project 2.3 can be determined. The result is shown in Table 2.10. The sums available from project 2.3 are FU 105 greater than those of project 2.1, i.e. the cash flow in year 5 of project 2.3.

TABLE 2.9
The cash flows of project 2.1 and project 2.3 (in FU's).

Year	Cash flow of project 2.1	Cash flow of project 2.3
1	(300)	(300)
2	170	170
3	140	140
4	105	105
5		105
Total	115	220
Earning power (%)	20	29.5

TABLE 2.10
A comparison of the available interest on outstanding balances of project 2.1, life time 4 years,[a] and project 2.3, life time 5 years (in FU's).

Year	Project 2.1 Interest = 20%	Project 2.3 Interest = 29.5%
1		
2	60	89
3	38	65
4	17	42
5		24
	115	220
Add:		
Investment	300	300
Positive cash flow	415	520

[a]See Table 2.2.

Therefore the earning power of project 2.3 is higher than that of project 2.1. The investment is the same in the two cases. This would mean that for projects with a longer life time a higher cost of capital is permissible.

If for any particular investment the rate of interest which is paid on loans is lower than the earning power, then cash surpluses are generated in the company. These surpluses can be used for one or a combination of the following purposes:

(1) reinvestment in new projects,
(2) paying dividends,
(3) adding to the liquid funds of the company,
(4) reinvestment in the money market.

However the earning power criterion does not imply that interest on loans will *in fact* be paid out of the cash generated by the new investment because the cash flow does not necessarily stay with the new investment during its life time. By relating the figures for the initial investment to the positive cash flow generated by it in later years, the criterion merely gives an indication of the profitability of the new investment. As such it is very useful. However it does not pretend that the financial details which are implied, will in fact be realised. Nor are the figures for individual years highlighted, because by its very nature earning power does not accept that; its essence is that is summarises in one figure a series of figures over a number of years. In the case of the financial accounts criterion, NI/NCE has meaning for individual years, and this is a great advantage. Earning power also isolates the new investment in the sense that the financial results are not related to those of the business as a whole.[2]

The criterion of present day value (PDV) is akin to that of earning power although it shows important differences. PDV is defined as the aggregate of the present day values of each of the annual cash flows at a given discount rate. It shows what surplus (either positive or negative) that cash flow would generate after it has been discounted at a given percentage. This is illustrated in Table 2.11.

Two elements of investment have to be paid out and have to earn interest on a reducing balance; the original investment of 300 and the present day value of 82. Each year the sums that are available from

[2]See Chapters 6 and 7.

TABLE 2.11
The calculation of the present day value of project 2.4 (in FU's).

Year	Cash flow	Discount factor (10%)	DCF
1	(300)	1	(300)
2	100	0.909	91
3	125	0.826	103
4	250	0.751	188
	175	Present day value	82

the cash flow for pay back of the elements of 300 and 82, are divided proportionately to them, as follows:

$$\text{Original investment:} \qquad \frac{300}{300 + 82} = 0.785,$$

$$\text{Present day value:} \qquad \frac{82}{300 + 82} = 0.215.$$

For example in year 2 a total of 62 is available for paying back the two elements, calculated as follows:

		FU's
	Cash flow year 2	100
Minus:	10% on outstanding investment of 300 in year 1	(30)
Minus:	10% interest on outstanding present day value of 82	(8)
		62

This is divided between pay back of the original sum of 300 and pay back of the present day value of 82 as follows:

H.P.J. Heukensfeldt Jansen

Pay back of the element of 300 : $62 \times 0.785 = 49$
Pay back of the element of   82 : $62 \times 0.215 = \underline{13}$

$\hspace{10cm}\underline{62}$

The following tables show the details for individual years:

Year	Towards paying out the original investment		FU's
2	$\dfrac{300}{(300 + 82)} = 0.785;$	$0.785 \times \ 62 =$	49
3		$0.785 \times \ 93 =$	73
4		$0.785 \times 227 =$	$\underline{178}$
			300

Year	Towards paying out present day value		FU's
2	$\dfrac{82}{(300 + 82)} = 0.215;$	$0.215 \times \ 62 =$	13
3		$0.215 \times \ 93 =$	20
4		$0.215 \times 227 =$	$\underline{49}$
			82

The final result is shown in Table 2.12.

Apart from paying out the original investment (= FU 300), see column 1, and accumulating the present day value (= FU 82), see column 4, interest on the outstanding investment, see column 3, and PDV, see column 6, has been earned (= FU 73 + FU 20). The total of:

	FU's
Original investment	= 300
Present day value	= 82
Interest 73 + 20	= 93
	475

is equal to the positive cash flow:

	FU's
Year 2	100
Year 3	125
Year 4	250
	475

It is clear that as in the case of earning power the interpretation of reducing balance can be applied to the criterion of present day value. However there is this difference that the (constant) return on the reducing balance applies not only to the original investment but also to the present day value of the aggregate cash flow.

Again as in the case of earning power, the criterion of present day value can be interpreted by taking literally the general formula for PDV. Compound interest is earned and it applies not only to the original investment but also to the present day value of the aggregate cash flow. Using the symbols already adopted the formula is:

$$\text{Present day value} = Q = -I + \frac{F_1}{1+R} + \frac{F_2}{(1+R)^2} + \frac{F_3}{(1+R)^3},$$

or:

$$I(1+R)^3 + Q(1+R)^3 = F_1(1+R)^2 + F_2(1+R) + F_3.$$

TABLE 2.12

The reducing balance interpretation of present day value for project 2.4 (in FU's).

Year	To pay-out investment (1)	Balance investment (2)	Interest on (2) 10% (3)
1		300	
2	49	251	30
3	73	178	25
4	178	0	18
Total	300		73

Year	To pay-out PDV (4)	Balance PDV (5)	Interest on (5) 10% (6)
1		82	
2	13	69	8
3	20	49	7
4	49	0	5
Total	82		20

Year	(1) + (4) = (7)	(3) + (6) = (8)	Positive CF (7) + (8) = (9)
1			
2	62	38	100
3	93	32	125
4	227	23	250
Total	382	93	475

Substituting the figures of the previous example into the formula this becomes:

$$300(1.1)^3 + 82(1.1)^3 = 100(1.1)^2 + 125(1.1) + 250.$$

The cash flow and the compound interest thereon yield sufficient funds to repay both the original investment and to accumulate a sum of money – the present day value. In addition funds are available to provide compound interest on the original investment and on the present day value, both at the selected rate of interest – or the rate of discount.

The most practical interpretation of the principle of present day value is that of compound interest. With its implications of the pay back of the present day value, and the interest on the outstanding balance thereof, the 'reducing balance' interpretation would indeed be cumbersome and very abstruse. In its normal applications the criterion establishes what surplus would be available after compound interest has been earned on the cash flow at a given rate of interest, or a given rate of discount. This is the compound interest interpretation. As such it is used to indicate what risks can be taken, e.g., if the cash flow is discounted at a very high rate of say 15% and there is still a positive PDV, then the project may be strong enough to weather the tides of adversity. Frequently the discount rate is related to, or equated to the assumed cost of capital. As in the case of earning power this implies that the length of the loan is equal to the life time of the project, and that the redemption pattern is in line.

As in the case of the criterion of earning power, the new investment looks more attractive the longer is the assumed life time of that investment. Therefore a PDV without a simultaneous specification of the life time of the new investment is meaningless. This is important because PDV's are almost exclusively used for comparative purposes.

Again the PDV criterion does not pretend that compound interest will *in fact* be generated by the cash flow of the project. The profitability assessment of the new investment by the criterion would apply whether or not the cash flow is in fact reinvested, or whether or not the cash flow continues to form part of the new investment.

The PDV criterion conceals the figures for individual years because as in the case of earning power it derives its meaning by summarising the financial results during the life time of the new investment into one figure. The new investment is also looked at in isolation without it being related in any way to the business as a whole. For discounted cash flow the new project is 'an' investment.

For ranking purposes the PDV criterion has (in contrast to the financial accounts criterion) the great advantage that it is simple, and therefore convenient to handle. It expresses the profitability of the new investment by relating the cash outgoing to the cash return, and the operation consists simply of discounting and adding a series of figures. The profitability is then expressed in one number and the size of that number is the criterion for the attractiveness of the investment. For ranking purposes two numbers are compared, and the highest one indicates the most attractive investment. Computers can easily be programmed to apply that principle, e.g., as a criterion for decision trees. This procedure has however formidable difficulties attached to it from the point of view of time preference (see Chapter 3).

By contrast a ranking of two investments by the criterion of the financial accounts is much more cumbersome. It consists of a number of operations, i.e.:

(1) subtracting the net income of the two alternatives from each other for each individual year;
(2) subtracting the net capital employed of the two alternatives from each other for each individual year;
(3) adding up the differential net incomes for the whole life time of the two investments;
(4) adding the differential net capital employed of the two investments for the whole life time of the two investments;
(5) dividing the total of the differential net income by the total of the differential net capital employed and then studying the resulting percentages.

Alternatively the differential net income as a percentage of the differential net capital employed can be studied for each individual year, which means comparing two series. Each series would have a considerable number of terms. In either case the procedure would be far longer than if the PDV criterion were used.

Summarising, for all practical purposes the two interpretations of the discounted cash flow do not apply symmetrically to the criteria of earning power and present day value. This is shown in Table 2.13.

TABLE 2.13
The most practical interpretation of earning power and present day value.

	Earning power	Present day value
Reducing balance interpretation	+	
Compound interest interpretation	−	+

It has been established that earning power indicates the upper limit of the rate of interest on any loans which the project can carry, and present day value gives an indication of the surplus which would be available after discounting the cash flow at a given discount rate. Frequently the criteria are related to the cost of capital, but seldom if ever is further attention given within that context to two very important facets of the cost of capital, the length of the loans and the redemption pattern. These are inextricably bound up with the structure of the cash flow. Therefore the use of the criteria of the discounted cash flow without quoting a life time is meaningless. Discounted cash flow also studies the new investment in isolation and conceals its financial return in individual years. The PDV criterion is a very convenient criterion for handling ranking problems but if it is used at all, the greatest care should be exercised and more information than only the PDV of the cash flow concerned is needed (see Chapter 3).

For project evaluation and the purpose for which project evaluation is carried out, the criteria of the discounted cash flow are useful but their value is certainly not outstanding. The following operations are involved in project evaluation:

(a) assembly of the basic data;
(b) completion of the necessary calculations;
(c) assessment of the resulting figures;
(d) a comparison afterwards of the actual results with the anticipated results – a post audit.

The purpose of project evaluation is:

(e) to assess the profitability of the new investment tel quel;

(f) to assess what difference the new investment will make over a
   period of years to the profit and loss account and balance sheet of
   the company as a whole.

Both earning power and PDV give an indication of the profitability
of the new investment per se (point e). However they do not give a
direct indication how the new investment would affect various major
parameters of the financial accounts (points c and f) notwithstanding
the fact that financial accounts are the scoreboard by which the financial performance of the company is assessed by its owners. If used to
the total exclusion of any other criterion, discounted cash flow is an
incomplete discipline in that, e.g., it ignores net income and by-passes
the need to think about new investments in terms of net income and
NI/NCE. The profitability performance of the project is measured as
though the new project were purely a cash transaction and as though
the cash generated by it, is the be all and end all of that investment.
There is no consideration of the future application of that cash by the
company, nor of its interdependence with the cash generated by the
existing business (see Chapter 6). If the cash is spent by the company
in any of the ways previously indicated then it can no longer be considered as part of the project because it is not available to the company as cash any longer. This means that the project would never
achieve in *a literal sense* the financial results indicated by, e.g., present
day value (even if all basic data had been correct and the future had
been accurately forecast), because the cash would not be available to
generate the compound interest which the concept implies. Nor would
the financial results of the project be entered into the books of the
company exactly as presented. In those senses the presuppositions
which the discounted cash flow implies would not materialise for a
new project. Therefore the criteria are abstract.
   By contrast if the profitability results of the new investment are expressed in terms identical to those of the company as a whole, then it
becomes possible:

(1) to relate the new investment to the existing business of which the
   results are reported in terms of financial accounts (see Chapters 6
   and 7);

(2) to establish afterwards how the financial results which were anticipated when the project was first submitted to the management for approval, have influenced the overall results of the business;[3]
(3) to compare the anticipated results with the actual results;
(4) to report on the anticipated financial results of the new investment in individual years.

Against that background the criteria of the discounted cash flow though they have their uses, become of secondary importance, because they are not directly relevant.

[3]However it may not always be simple to separate out the financial results of the new project those of the company as a whole.

CHAPTER 3

DISCOUNTED CASH FLOW AND TIME PREFERENCE

An important advantage which is always quoted in favour of dis-counted cash flow is, that it gives preference to an *early* cash flow. This is well known. However if PDV is taken as the profitability criterion for the selection of mutually exclusive alternatives and pay-out time is taken as the criterion for an early or a late cash flow, then PDV may result in the cash flow with the longest pay-out time being selected. This is apparently not generally known.

With regard to earning power,[4] it may be said that at a given *un-discounted* aggregate of a cash flow, the earning power of that cash flow (i.e., the discount rate at which its PDV $= 0$) is greater, the *earlier* the incidence of that cash flow. An example is given in Table 3.1. The accrual of the cash flow through time is earlier for cash flow 3.1 than for cash flow 3.2. Consequently the earning power of cash flow 3.1 is higher. The same holds true for the criterion of PDV in this case, and the PDV of the early cash flow is greater than that of the late cash flow (see also later Case 1).

However it should be noted that the undiscounted aggregates of cash flows 3.1 and 3.2 are equal ($=$ FU 57). If they are not equal then the relationship between the size of the PDV and time preference is more complicated. It is even possible to construct two cash flows of which the later one has the higher PDV but correspondingly a lower earning power (see Table 3.2). Although cash flow 3.3 (early) has an earning power of 16% whilst cash flow 3.4 (late) has an earning power of 13%, cash flow 3.4 (late) has the higher PDV at discount rates of 6%, 8% and 10%. This should be contrasted with cash flows 3.1

---

[4]For a definition of earning power and present day value, see Chapter 2.

TABLE 3.1
Earning power and the timing of the cash flow (in FU's).

Year	Cash flow 3.1 (early)	Cash flow 3.2 (late)
1	(300)	(400)
2	200	250
3	119	169
4	38	38
Total	57	57
EP (%)	12	9
PDV (6%)	25	17
POT (years)	2.8	2.9

(early) and 3.2 (late) in which cash flow 3.1 (early) has both a higher earning power and a higher PDV (see Table 3.1). It shows that a systematic analysis of the relationship between time preference and the size of the PDV is needed.

TABLE 3.2
PDV and the timing of the cash flow (in FU's).

Year	Cash flow 3.3 (early)	Cash flow 3.4 (late)
1	(1000)	(1000)
2	935	(100)
3	180	55
4	50	350
5	30	600
6	25	800
PDV 0%	220	705
6%	120	303
8%	91	200
10%	65	111
EP (%)	16	13
POT (years)	2.4	5.1

The most practical way of defining an early and a late cash flow is with reference to the relationship between the size of the investment and the size of the positive cash flow which is generated by that investment in the years immediately after the investment has been made, i.e., the pay-out time (POT).

In the definition of the various cases which will be studied the following parameters of the early cash flow (ECF) and late cash flow (LCF) should be distinguished.

(1) *The undiscounted cash flow, i.e., the PDV at %.* The undiscounted aggregate of the early and late cash flows may be equal, i.e.,

PDV 0%:   ECF = LCF,

or the early cash flow may have a greater undiscounted aggregate cash flow than the late cash flow, i.e.,

PDV 0%:   ECF > LCF,

or it may have a smaller undiscounted aggregate cash flow, i.e.,

PDV 0%:   ECF < LCF.

(2) *The earning power.* The earning power of the early cash flow may be equal to that of the late cash flow, i.e.,

EP: ECF = LCF,

or it may be greater than that of the late cash flow, i.e.,

EP: ECF > LCF,

or it may be smaller, i.e.,

EP: ECF < LCF.

An important part is played by the differential cash flow, because the PDV curves of two cash flows meet at a discount rate which is equal to the earning power of the differential cash flow.

For most practical applications the PDV curves of two projects will only meet once and will only cross the X-axis once. Exceptions can be found but the rule applies to the majority of realistic cases where the weight of expenditure is concentrated in the early years, and these are the cases which will be considered.

Although PDV's which are initially negative, have no practical financial significance, they can be used as a device for dealing with ranking problems. For that reason they will not be ignored.

Negative discount factors will not be considered because they are unrealistic.

For a summary of the cases which will be studied see Table 3.10. The cases are not equally likely to occur but a complete analysis has been given so as to give the reader a better insight into the problem. Cases 5–8 are the most realistic.

The following symbols and abbreviations have been used:

E	Earning power early cash flow.
L	Earning power late cash flow.
D	Earning power differential cash flow.
EP	Earning power.
CF	Cash flow.
ECF	Early cash flow.
LCF	Late cash flow.

Case 1

Assumptions:

PDV 0%:   ECF = LCF,
EP: ECF > LCF.

The case is illustrated by a numerical example (see Table 3.3 and Graph 3.1).

TABLE 3.3
Case 1 (in FU's).

Year		Cash flow 3.1 (early)	Cash flow 3.5 (late)	Differential
1		(300)	(400)	100
2		200	250	(50)
3		119	169	(50)
4		38	38	0
PDV	0%	57	57	0
	4%	34	29	5
	8%	16	6	10
	10%	8	(4)	12
	12%	0	(13)	13
	16%	(13)	(30)	17
EP	%	12	9	0
POT	(years)	2.8	2.9	

The earning power of the differential cash flow is equal to zero, i.e.,

$$D = 0,$$

because it has been assumed that the undiscounted cash flows are equal. Therefore the curves of the early and late cash flow cross on the Y-axis.

The PDV's of the early cash flow are greater than those of the late cash flow. Therefore, the PDV's favour an early cash flow at all discount rates except 0.

Case 2

Assumptions:

> PDV 0%: ECF = LCF,
> EP: ECF < LCF.

This case is unrealistic.

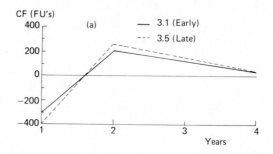

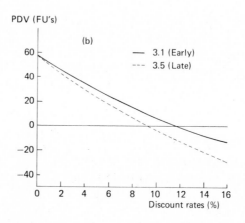

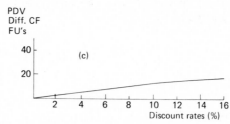

Graph 3.1. *Case 1.* (a) A comparison of the time profile of cash flows 3.1 (early) and 3.5 (late). (b) The PDV's of cash flows 3.1 (early) and 3.5 (late) at various discount rates. (c) The PDV's of the differential cash flow at various discount rates.

Case 3

Assumptions:

PDV 0%:   ECF > LCF,
EP: ECF = LCF.

The case is illustrated by a numerical example (see Table 3.4 and Graph 3.2).

TABLE 3.4
Case 3 (in FU's).

Year		Cash flow 3.1 (early)	Cash flow 3.6 (late)	Differential
1		(300)	(77)	(223)
2		200	(50)	250
3		119	119	0
4		38	38	0
PDV	0%	57	30	27
	4%	34	18	16
	8%	16	8	8
	10%	8	4	4
	12%	0	0	0
	16%	(13)	(6)	(7)
EP	%	12	12	12
POT	(years)	2.8	3.2	

The earning power of the differential cash flow is equal to the earning powers of the early and late cash flows. The PDV curves of the early and late cash flows cross the *X*-axis on the same point. Thus,

$$E = L = D.$$

The PDV curve of the early cash flow meets the *Y*-axis at a higher point than the PDV curve of the late cash flow. Therefore, at discount

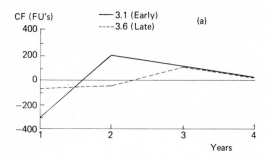

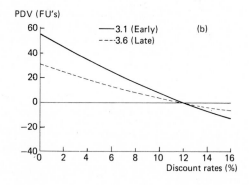

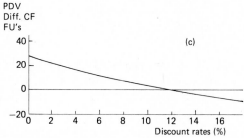

Graph 3.2. *Case 3.* (a) A comparison of the time profile of cash flows 3.1 (early) and 3.6 (late). (b) The PDV's of cash flows 3.1 (early) and 3.6 (late) at various discount rates. (c) The PDV's of the differential cash flow at various discount rates.

rates smaller than D the PDV's favour an early cash flow, and at discount rates greater than D the PDV's favour a late cash flow.

Case 4

Assumptions:

$$PDV\ 0\%:\ ECF < LCF,$$
$$EP:\qquad ECF = LCF.$$

The case is illustrated by a numerical example (see Table 3.5 and Graph 3.3).

As in Case 3 the earning power of the differential cash flow is equal to the earning powers of the early and late cash flows. Again the PDV curves of the early and late cash flows cross the X-axis on the same point. Thus,

$$E = L = D.$$

TABLE 3.5
Case 4 (in FU's).

Year		Cash flow 3.1 (early)	Cash flow 3.7 (late)	Differential
1		(300)	(170)	(130)
2		200	(220)	420
3		119	210	(91)
4		38	280	(242)
PDV	0%	57	100	(43)
	4%	34	59	(25)
	8%	16	27	(11)
	10%	8	13	(5)
	12%	0	0	0
	16%	(13)	(21)	8
EP	(%)	12	12	12
POT	(years)	2.8	3.6	

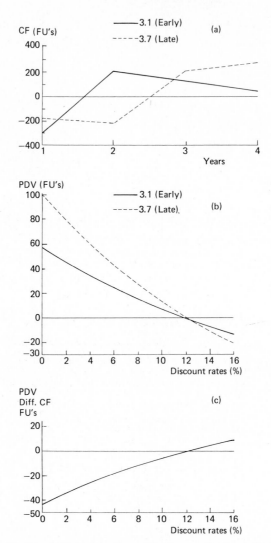

Graph 3.3. *Case 4.* (a) A comparison of the time profile of cash flows 3.1 (early) and 3.7 (late). (b) The PDV's of cash flows 3.1 (early) and 3.7 (late) at various discount rates. (c) The PDV's of the differential cash flow at various discount rates.

The PDV curve of the late cash flow meets the Y-axis at a higher point than the PDV curve of the early cash flow. Therefore, at discount rates smaller than D the PDV's favour a late cash flow, and at discount rates greater than D the PDV's favour an early cash flow.

Case 5

Assumptions:

$$
\begin{aligned}
&\text{PDV } 0\%: \ \text{ECF} > \text{LCF,} \\
&\text{EP:} \qquad \text{ECF} > \text{LCF.}
\end{aligned}
$$

The case is illustrated by a numerical example (see Table 3.6 and Graph 3.4).

The earning power of the differential cash flow is greater than that

TABLE 3.6
Case 5 (in FU's).

Year		Cash flow 3.1 (early)	Cash flow 3.8 (late)	Differential
1		(300)	(77)	(223)
2		200	50	250
3		119	75	44
4		38	80	(42)
PDV	0%	57	28	29
	4%	34	15	19
	8%	16	4	12
	10%	8	0	8
	12%	0	(5)	5
	16%	(13)	(11)	(2)
	18%	(18)	(14)	(4)
EP	(%)	12	10	15
POT	(years)	2.8	3.7	

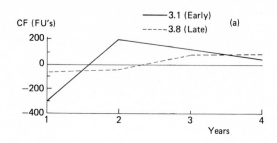

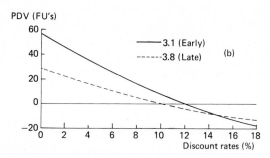

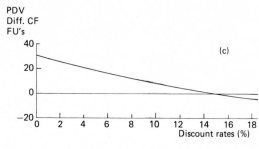

Graph 3.4. *Case 5.* (a) A comparison of the time profile of cash flows 3.1 (early) and 3.8 (late). (b) The PDV's of cash flows 3.1 (early) and 3.8 (late) at various discount rates. (c) The PDV's of the differential cash flow at various discount rates.

of the early and late cash flow. Thus,

$$D > E,$$
$$D > L.$$

The undiscounted total of the early and late cash flows is positive. Therefore the PDV at the point where the PDV curves of the early and late cash flows meet is negative.

The PDV curve of the early cash flow meets the Y-axis at a higher point than the PDV curve of the late cash flow. Therefore, at discount rates smaller than D the present day values favour an early cash flow, and at discount rates greater than D the present day values favour a late cash flow.

Case 6

Assumptions:

$$\text{PDV } 0\%: \quad \text{ECF} < \text{LCF},$$
$$\text{EP:} \qquad \text{ECF} > \text{LCF}.$$

The case is illustrated by a numerical example (see Table 3.7 and Graph 3.5).

The earning power of the differential cash flow is smaller than that of the early and late cash flow. Thus,

$$D < E,$$
$$D < L.$$

The undiscounted total of the early and late cash flows is positive. Therefore the PDV at the point where the early and late cash flows meet is positive.

The PDV curve of the late cash flow meets the Y-axis at a higher point than the PDV curve of the early cash flow. Therefore, at discount rates smaller than D the PDV's favour a late cash flow, and at count rates smaller than D the PDV's favour a late cash flow, and at

TABLE 3.7
Case 6 in (FU's).

Year		Cash flow 3.1 (early)	Cash flow 3.9 (late)	Differential
1		(300)	(167)	(133)
2		200	(220)	420
3		119	214	(95)
4		38	253	(215)
PDV	0%	57	80	(23)
	4%	34	42	(8)
	7%	20	19	1
	10%	8	0	8
	12%	0	(11)	11
	16%	(13)	(31)	18
EP	(%)	12	10	7
POT	(years)	2.8	3.7	

discount rates greater than D the PDV's favour an early cash flow.

Case 7

Assumptions:

$$PDV\ 0\%:\quad ECF > LCF,$$
$$EP:\qquad\quad ECF < LCF.$$

The case is illustrated by a numerical example (see Table 3.8 and Graph 3.6).

The earning power of the differential cash flow is smaller than that of the early and late cash flows. Thus,

$$D < E,$$
$$D < L.$$

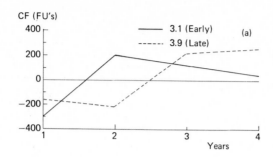

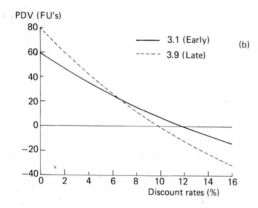

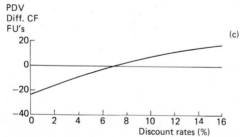

Graph 3.5. *Case 6*. (a) A comparison of the time profile of cash flows 3.1 (early) and 3.9 (late). (b) The PDV's of cash flows 3.1 (early) and 3.9 (late) at various discount rates. (c) The PDV's of the differential cash flow at various discount rates.

H.P.J. Heukensfeldt Jansen

TABLE 3.8
Case 7 (in FU's).

Year		Cash flow 3.1 (early)	Cash flow 3.10 3.10 (late)	Differential
1		(300)	(77)	(223)
2		200	(50)	250
3		119	86	33
4		38	81	(43)
PDV	0%	57	40	17
	4%	34	25	9
	9%	12	11	1
	10%	8	9	(1)
	12%	0	4	(4)
	14%	(7)	0	(7)
	16%	(13)	(4)	(9)
EP	(%)	12	14	10
POT	(years)	2.8	3.5	

The undiscounted total of the early and late cash flows is positive. Therefore the PDV at the point where the PDV curves of the early and late cash flows meet is positive.

The PDV curve of the early cash flow meets the Y-axis at a higher point than the PDV curve of the late cash flow. Therefore, at discount rates smaller than D the PDV's favour an early cash flow, and at discount rates greater than D the PDV's favour a late cash flow.

Case 8

Assumptions:

$$\text{PDV 0\%:} \quad \text{ECF} < \text{LCF,}$$
$$\text{EP:} \quad \text{ECF} < \text{LCF.}$$

The case is illustrated by a numerical example (see Table 3.9 and Graph 3.7).

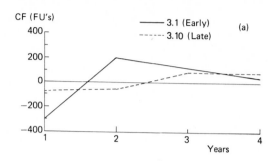

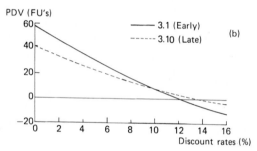

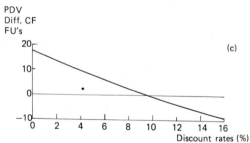

Graph 3.6. *Case 7.* (a) A comparison of the time profile of cash flows 3.1 (early) and 3.10 (late). (b) The PDV's of cash flows 3.1 (early) and 3.10 (late) at various discount rates. (c) The PDV's of the differential cash flow at various discount rates.

TABLE 3.9
Case 8 (in FU's).

Year		Cash flow 3.1 (early)	Cash flow 3.11 (late)	Differential
1		(300)	(330)	30
2		200	165	35
3		119	152	(33)
4		38	94	(56)
PDV	0%	57	81	(24)
	4%	34	50	(16)
	8%	16	26	(10)
	12%	0	5	(5)
	13%	(3)	0	(3)
	16%	(13)	(13)	0
	20%	(24)	(27)	3
EP	(%)	12	13	16
POT	(years)	2.8	3.1	

The earning power of the differential cash flow is greater than that of the early and late cash flows. Thus,

$$D > E,$$
$$D > L.$$

The undiscounted total of the early and late cash flows is positive. Therefore the PDV at the point where the PDV curves of the early and late cash flows meet is negative.

The PDV curve of the late cash flow meets the Y-axis at a higher point than the PDV curve of the early cash flow. Therefore, at discount rates smaller than D the PDV's favour a late cash flow, and at discount rates greater than D the PDV's favour an early cash flow.

The results of Cases 1–8 are summarised in Table 3.10.

It will be seen that by taking a positive discount factor and comparing the PDV's of two alternatives (not ignoring negative ones) the evaluator has about a 50/50 chance that he selects a project with the

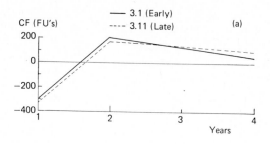

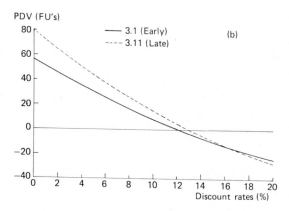

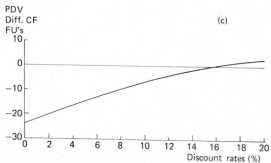

Graph 3.7. *Case 8.* (a) A comparison of the time profile of cash flows 3.1 (early) and 3.11 (late). (b) The PDV's of cash flows 3.1 (early) and 3.11 (late) at various discount rates. (c) The PDV's of the differential cash flow at various discount rates.

TABLE 3.10
PDV and the timing up of the cash flow.[a]

Case	PDV 0%	EP	Time preference at discount rates	
			< D	> D
1	ECF = LCF	ECF > LCF	—	early
2	ECF = LCF	ECF < LCF	—	—
3	ECF > LCF	ECF = LCF	early	late
4	ECF < LCF	ECF = LCF	late	early
5	ECF > LCF	ECF > LCF	early	late
6	ECF < LCF	ECF > LCF	late	early
7	ECF > LCF	ECF < LCF	early	late
8	ECF < LCF	ECF < LCF	late	early

[a]*Abbreviations:* PDV: present day value, EP: earning power, *D*: earning power differential cash flow, ECF: early cash flow, LCF: late cash flow.

shorter pay-out time. A PDV may reflect a high earning power which is favourable but also a late cash flow which is unfavourable. From this point of view the difference between the PDV's of two alternatives is not necessarily an indication of the comparative merits of the alternatives because a high PDV may be associated with a late cash flow. Furthermore the size of the difference may reflect the level of the discount rate. All things being equal the PDV criterion selects at discount rates smaller than *D*, the project with the highest capital expenditure.

It follows that PDV is by itself an insufficient criterion for ranking purposes. If the criterion is to be used at all, it is highly advisable also to work out further information on the two alternatives.

From this information an advisable discount factor for the calculation of the PDV's of the two alternatives can then be selected, i.e., the discount rate *follows*. The following operations are required:

(1) Calculate the pay-out time of the two alternatives.
(2) Calculate the aggregate of the undiscounted cash flows of the two alternatives.
(3) Calculate the earning power of the differential cash flow of the two alternatives.

(4) Calculate the earning power of the two alternatives.
(5) Calculate the PDV's at an advisable discount rate of the two alternatives.

The use of the PDV criterion is not so simple after all and certainly not as simple as it would appear to be from Chapter 2. It may be said that the proper application of the PDV criterion for selection purposes is as lengthy and troublesome as that of earning power or the financial accounts criterion and then one may as well work out and study the financial accounts criteria in the first place. The problems into which a blind use of the PDV criterion may lead the evaluator are discussed in Chapter 5, but before then a close examination of the relationship of the discounted cash flow and net income is needed. This will be done in Chapter 4.

CHAPTER 4

NET INCOME AND CASH FLOW

Net income clearly plays a major part in the assessment by the market of the success of the business. It is therefore only logical that it is worked out for new investments. Just as the success of a football match is measured in terms of goals and therefore the team's manager will not instruct the players to get as many corners as possible, although corners may easily lead to goals; thus the success of the business is measured in terms of net income (loss) and net income in relation to the investment needed to achieve it, i.e., net income as a % of net capital employed. Success is not measured in a direct way in cash flow although success in cash flow may easily but not necessarily, lead to success in net income.

There seems to be an overwhelmingly logical case for working out net income because that is what any business tries to achieve. Yet although few people disagree that the maintenance of a certain minimum net income must be the ultimate objective of business in order to survive, the cash flow specialists stop short of working it out when a new investment is being studied. It is even felt to be slightly old-fashioned to work out net income in project evaluation. The cash flow concept has become very generally accepted and can be said to be truly in fashion. It is as though one were planning to fly from *A* to *B*, and one were accused of using old-fashioned methods by setting course direct to *B*. The author of this study would rather be called old-fashioned than illogical.

What then is the relationship between cash flow and the results of the business as they would appear in the books of the company? Would any harm be done to the company by working out solely the cash flow of a new investment, whilst ignoring net income?

The relationship between net income and cash flow is a relationship over time; although the figures for cash flow may be divergent from those of net income in individual years, their aggregate during the life time of the project should be equal. In simple terms, if in a cash flow calculation 'everything is substracted from everything else', the total of net income should be obtained. Therefore a cash flow calculation and the corresponding net income calculation are in balance if the following equation is satisfied:

$$\sum_{0}^{L} \text{cash flow} = \sum_{0}^{L} \text{net income},$$

whereby L is the life time of the project.

For project 'P' the build-up of the two totals is shown in Table 4.1.

TABLE 4.1

The relationship between the cash flow and net income for project 'P', life time 22 years (in FU's).

	Total for years 1–22	
	Net income	Cash flow
1. Cash before tax after stock build-up	41,185.8	41,185.8
2. Capital expenditure/ depreciation	(7,461.0)	(7,461.0)
3. Tax	(17,020.1)	(17,020.1)
4. Debtors		(862.4)
5. Other working capital		(339.2)
6. Stocks	314.9	314.9[a]
7. Debtors		862.4[a]
8. Other working capital		339.2[a]
Total	17,019.6	17,019.6

[a]The total of items 6, 7 and 8 is equal to FU 1516.5 which is the residual value of the cash flow (see footnote c to Table 1.1).

Net income is calculated by substracting from the netback, the costs incurred for manufacturing sales quantities and this excludes the costs of manufacturing stocks. However in the example of project 'P' (see Tables 1.1 and 1.2) the total of the variable and fixed costs (lines 6, 7 and 9) and the total of depreciation (line 25) which includes those for making stocks, have been substracted in the first instance. Therefore the stock valuation, i.e., the costs incurred for making stocks have to be added back if a correct computation of net income is to be made. This has been done (see line 26 in Table 1.2 and line 6 in Table 4.1).

By contrast a cash flow is arrived at by subtracting from the net-back all costs including those for stock build-up, and the depreciation element for making stocks is included in capital expenditure (see line 17 in Table 1.1). In other words in a cash flow calculation stocks should be added back if there is to be equality between the total of the cost elements which go into a net income computation and those which go into a cash flow calculation. This is done not by adding back stocks in individual years by the amounts of the increases (decreases) in those years as in a net income calculation, but by assuming that the cumulative total of stocks outstanding at the end of the period is cashed in – in the case of project 'P' in year 22. Thus there is a positive addition to the cash flow for that amount in year 22.

The depreciation during the life time of the project is of course equal to the total of capital expenditure (see line 17 in Table 1.1 and line 2 in Table 4.1). The difference between the treatment of deprecia-tion and capital expenditure in a cash flow and a net income computa-tion is, that in a cash flow calculation capital expenditure is sub-stracted as and when it occurs (see year 1 to 3, line 17 in Table 1.1) whilst in a net income calculation it is 'artificially' spread out as a book entry during a number of years after the plant has started opera-tions. The treatment of capital expenditure in a cash flow and in a net income calculation could be compared with the spreading of butter on a slice of bread; in a cash flow calculation butter is put on the slice in a number of lumps (i.e., in the amounts and at the time expenditure is in-curred), whilst in the net income calculation butter is spread out either evenly (linear depreciation) or at a progressively declining rate (declin-ing balance).

Debtors and 'other' working capital do not appear in a net income calculation. However in a cash flow calculation they have to be subtracted from the netback as and when they are built up over the years, because otherwise a true cash position for individual years would not result. This means again that these items have to be added back in a cash flow calculation if equality between the total of net income and the total cash flow both during the life time of the project, is to result. It is done by assuming that the cumulative totals are cashed in as a lump sum at the end of the period – in the case of project 'P' in year 22 – resulting in an addition to the positive cash flow in that year. From footnote c to Table 1.1 it can also be seen that the total of the cash flow from years 1–22 (FU 17,019.6) has been arrived at by adding a residual value of FU 1516.5 consisting entirely of working capital to the aggregate of the cash flows of the years 1–22. In lines 6, 7 and 8 of Table 4.1 the amounts for stocks, debtors and 'other' working capital which make up this total, are separately given.

The foregoing means in effect that in building up a cash flow a very important assumption has to be made, i.e., that the new project has a life time at the end of which it is liquidated with its attendant operations; for cashing in of working capital makes no sense unless it is simultaneously assumed that the whole operation is liquidated when the end of its life time has come.

It may well be asked whether in working out a cash flow it can be assumed that working capital is not cashed in at all or at a price lower than the cost of manufacture, or at a price higher than the cost of manufacture. Of course it can. It would however necessitate a corresponding adjustment in the profit and loss account respectively a loss, or an addition to net income. For example, in the case of project 'P' (see Tables 1.1 and 1.2), the working capital is cashed in at its historic cost/value, i.e., at FU 1516.5. If it were to be cashed in at say FU 1000 there would be a loss of FU 516.5. This would be subtracted from the total of net income over the period and the formula

$$\sum_{0}^{L} \text{cash flow} = \sum_{0}^{L} \text{net income}$$

would again be satisfied.

The following situations may occur:

Discounted cash flow	Consequence for profit and loss account
Working capital is cashed in at a price:	
(1) above manufacturing cost	Addition to net income
(2) equal to manufacturing cost	No consequence
(3) below manufacturing cost or at a price = 0, i.e., not cashed in at all	Loss

If the evaluator uses the discipline of the discounted cash flow he would have to report in Cases 1 and 3 in addition to the earning power and PDV of the cash flow, the fact that there would be an addition to net income – or a loss – on working capital at the end of the period, i.e., he would have to resort to a discipline in which evaluations are made in terms of net income and net capital employed, 'the financial accounts profitability criteria', and this discipline is extraneous to that of the discounted cash flow. In fact the technique of the discounted cash flow has been designed so as to avoid the use of exactly those criteria because it avoids book entries (of depreciation). Only in case 2 in which working capital is cashed in at its historic cost/value is there no necessity for their application. In other words the cash flow method of project evaluation in its *pure* form, *commits* the evaluator to make two assumptions whether he believes them or not, that

(1) all working capital is cashed in,
(2) all working capital is cashed in at its historic cost/value.

Yet to some this may sound too puristic, and an adjustment to the value of the cashed in working capital at the end of the period in terms of the profit and loss account, and balance sheet, may be considered acceptable from the point of view of methodology. The point is that the cash flow discipline forces the evaluator to make an assumption that working capital will be cashed in, and the evaluator may not wish to do so. Thus the evaluator may wish to assume that no working capital will be cashed in at all, and he may reject the methodological implications to which the technique of the discounted cash flow commit him.

Re-examining the above spectrum of options which are open for handling, the evaluator may have comments as indicated:

Assumptions	*Comments of the evaluator*
(1) Working capital is cashed in at a price above or below the historic cost/value.	He may not be prepared to believe that working capital is to be cashed in at all; or he may not be prepared to assume that there is a profit or loss on this account at the end of the period.
(2) Working capital is cashed in at a price equal to the historic cost/value.	He may not be prepared to believe that working capital is to be cashed in.
(3) Working capital is not cashed in and no loss adjustment on the profit and loss account is foreseen.	He may wish to make these assumptions but by its very nature the method of the discounted cash flow does not allow them to be introduced.

The assumptions of Case 3 would not be unrealistic or unlikely to occur. An example would be the profitability evaluation of a machine for the manufacture of a product which has shown a steadily increasing demand in the past and is expected to continue this trend in future. It may therefore not be considered realistic to assume that working capital will be cashed in at the end of the life time of that machine, because far from being cashed in, working capital has shown a steadily rising trend over the years, in line with growth in demand, and as and when machines were replaced or their number was increased. As cashing in has not occurred in the past it is not expected to happen in future. Cases like these are known to the author.

Thus there are very considerable differences in the treatment of capital expenditure and working capital by the financial accounts analysis on the one hand, and the cash flow analysis on the other hand, and yet the aggregate of the cash flow and the corresponding net income during the life time of the investment are equal. In view of this, it is not surprising that there is a divergency in the time profile of net income and the corresponding cash flow. This is illustrated for project 'P' (see Table 1.1) in Graph 4.1, where the net income and cash flow, and the corresponding cumulative totals are shown through time. It will be seen that one year after the plant starts operations the cash flow remains much at the same level. When the plant is fully written off the cash flow falls but net income rises. At the end of the life time of the project working capital is cashed in and forms part of the cash flow curve. Thus the cumulative cash flow which has been at a lower level than the cumulative net income from years 2–22, reaches the same level as cumulative net income in year 23, but it does so along an entirely different route.

The differences in time profile are further illustrated in Graph 4.2 where the NI/NCE and the cash flow of project 'P' are compared. Here again the data which are assessed in the cash flow and financial accounts profitability disciplines, namely cash flow and NI/NCE, show an entirely different time profile and their relative slope should be particularly noted. The cash flow reaches a plateau very much sooner than the NI/NCE, and the NI/NCE rises steadily as the plant is written off and reaches a plateau when the plant is fully depreciated. The cash flow curve however falls to a lower level when the plant is fully written off.

It has been noted that the differences in time profile arise because the cash flow and financial accounts techniques of analysis treat capital expenditure and working capital very differently. It is therefore appropriate to compare two identical cash flows which conceal different proportions of fixed investment and working capital, and then

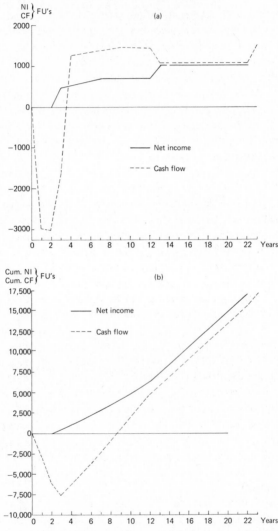

Graph 4.1. (a) A comparison of the time profile of the cash flow and net income of project 'P'. (b) A comparison of the time profile of the cumulative cash flow and cumulative net income of project 'P'. (See for project 'P' Tables 1.1 and 1.2.)

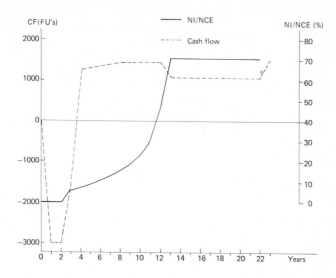

Graph 4.2. A comparison of the time profile of the cash flow and net income/net capital employed of project 'P'. (See Tables 1.1 and 1.2.)

to explore what effect this has on the financial accounts criteria.

The capital investment of project 4.1 (high working capital) and project 4.2 (low working capital) is identical (= FU 1000), and so is the remainder of the cash flow (see Table 4.2). However the components of the investment are different: whilst the proportion of working capital to fixed investment is 20 ÷ 100 for project 4.1 (high working capital) it is 1 ÷ 99 for project 4.2 (low working capital). From year 2 the first year of operation only the cash generation and fixed investment (in the form of depreciation) enter into the net income computation (see Table 4.3). From year 2 to year 11 the cash generation of the two cases is equal (= cash flow) but the depreciation of project 4.1 (high working capital) is lower than that of project 4.2 (low working capital). Consequently the net income of project 4.1 (high working capital) is higher in years 2–11 than that of project 4.2 (low working capital).

H.P.J. Heukensfeldt Jansen

TABLE 4.2

A comparison of the cash flows of project 4.1 (high working capital) and project 4.2 (low working capital) (in FU's).[a]

Year	Project 4.1 (High working capital)				Project 4.2 (Low working capital)			
	Cash gen.	Capital exp.	Working cap.	Cash flow	Cash gen.	Capital exp.	Working cap.	Cash flow
1	—	(833)	(167)	(1000)	—	(990)	(10)	(1000)
2	120			120	120			120
3	130			130	130			130
4	150			150	150			150
5	167			167	167			167
6	167			167	167			167
7	167			167	167			167
8	167			167	167			167
9	167			167	167			167
10	167			167	167			167
11	167			167	167			167
12			167	167	157		10	167
Total				736				736

[a]Earning power = 10%.

The profile through time of the net income of the two cases, and the cash flow is illustrated in Graph 4.3. The net income of project 4.1 (high working capital) is higher than that of project 4.2 (low working capital), and also closer to the cash flow curve in years 2–11. This is also the case for the cumulative figures where again the curve for project 4.1 (high working capital) is above that of project 4.2 (low working capital). Thus the differential net income shows a positive balance in favour of project 4.2 (high working capital) until year 11. This situation is reversed in year 12 when the cash flow of project 4.2 (high working capital) is generated entirely by cashing in the working capital; thus the cash generation = 0. The cash flow of project 4.2 (low working capital) consists in the same year of two elements: cash generation (FU 157) and cashing in working capital (FU 10).

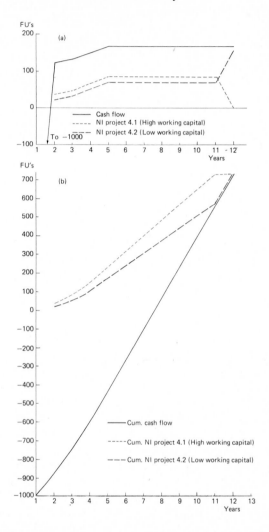

Graph 4.3. (a) The cash flow and net income of project 4.1 (high working capital) and project 4.2 (low working capital). (b) The cumulative cash flow and net income of the same projects.

TABLE 4.3

A comparison of the net income of project 4.1 (high working capital) and
project 4.2 (low working capital) (in FU's).

Year	Project 4.1 (High working capital)			Project 4.2 (Low working capital)		
	Cash generation	Depreciation	Net income	Cash generation	Depreciation	Net income
1						
2	120	(83)	37	120	(99)	21
3	130	(83)	47	130	(99)	31
4	150	(84)	66	150	(99)	51
5	167	(83)	84	167	(99)	68
6	167	(83)	84	167	(99)	68
7	167	(84)	83	167	(99)	68
8	167	(83)	84	167	(99)	68
9	167	(83)	84	167	(99)	68
10	167	(84)	83	167	(99)	68
11	167	(83)	84	167	(99)	68
12			0	157		157
Total			736			736

Therefore in year 12 when the fixed investment is fully written off in both cases, the net income of project 4.2 (low working capital) is FU 157 whilst that of project 4.1 (high working capital) is 0. The cumulative net income curve of project 4.2 (low working capital) which has been below that of project 4.1 (high working capital) over the whole period, catches up in year 12 as the result of the net income being much higher in that year. And then it reaches of course the same point as the cumulative net income of project 4.1 (high working capital) and the cumulative cash flow. For identical cash flows in that year the net income situation is profoundly affected by the fact that a relatively high working capital is realised in case 4.1 (high working capital) and a relatively low one in case 4.2 (low working capital).

The net capital employed of project 4.1 (high working capital) is higher than that of project 4.2 (low working capital) in all years except in year 1 and year 12 when they are equal (see Table 4.4). These differences arise notwithstanding the fact that on a cash flow basis the investment is equal in the two cases (=FU 1000).

TABLE 4.4

A comparison of the net capital employed of project 4.1 (high working capital) and project 4.2 (low working capital) (in FU's).

Year	Project 4.1 (High working capital)			Project 4.2 (Low working capital)		
	Book value	Working capital	NCE	Book value	Working capital	NCE
1	833	167	1000	990	10	1000
2	750	167	917	891	10	901
3	667	167	834	792	10	802
4	583	167	750	693	10	703
5	500	167	667	594	10	604
6	417	167	584	495	10	505
7	333	167	500	396	10	406
8	250	167	417	297	10	307
9	167	167	334	198	10	208
10	83	167	250	99	10	109
11	0	167	167	0	10	10
12	0	0	0	0	0	0

Working capital is not written off. The higher working capital plus the lower book value of project 4.1 (high working capital) result in a higher net capital employed, because it is higher than the lower working capital plus the higher book value of project 4.2 (low working capital). It should be noted that the difference in the net capital employed increases as the end of the life time of the project is approached.

The net result of the difference in net income and net capital employed of the two cases is, that the NI/NCE of project 4.1 (high working capital) in years 2–6 is higher than that of case 4.2 (low working capital) whilst in years 7–12 it is lower (see Table 4.5).

TABLE 4.5

A comparison of the NI/NCE of project 4.1 (high working capital) and project 4.2
(low working capital) and the differential NI/NCE (in %)

Year	NI/NCE (%)		
	Project 4.1 (High working capital)	Project 4.2 (Low working capital)	Difference
1			
2	4.0	2.3	100.0
3	5.6	3.8	50.0
4	8.8	7.2	31.9
5	12.6	11.2	25.4
6	14.4	13.4	20.3
7	16.6	16.7	15.9
8	20.1	22.1	14.5
9	25.1	32.6	12.7
10	33.2	62.3	10.6
11	50.3	680.0	10.2
12	—	∞	$(-\infty)$

However in spite of the fact that it is lower in those years, project 4.1 (high working capital) still shows a fairly high NI/NCE of over 10% on the marginal net capital employed, and this may well be acceptable. Graph 4.4 shows that the differential NI/NCE falls steadily from year 1 to year 11 starting at 100% in year 2 and becoming infinite (negative) in year 12. The differential NI/NCE is only reversed in favour of project 4.2 (low working capital) in year 12 when working capital is cashed in.

Although the two projects are equally acceptable by the criterion of the discounted cash flow (if at least 10% earning power as a cut-off point is acceptable) they are certainly very different in terms of book profitability.

There is a very strong case for making project 4.1 (high working capital) the preferred choice but the question of cashing in of working capital needs special attention. If realisation of working capital plays an important role, as it does in this case, it deserves further analysis for its validity in the light of the circumstances. It is therefore un-desirable to conceal it under the one summarising figure of earning

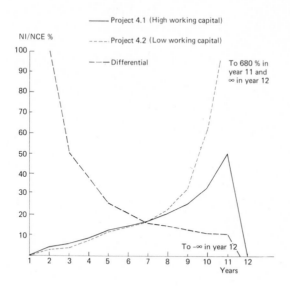

NI/NCE %

———— Project 4.1 (High working capital)

---- Project 4.2 (Low working capital)

— — — Differential

To 680 % in year 11 and ∞ in year 12

To –∞ in year 12

Years

Graph 4.4. A comparison of the net income as a percentage of the net capital employed of project 4.1 (high working capital) and project 4.2 (low working capital) and the differential NI/NCE.

power or PDV. The realisation of working capital does not play an integral part in the financial accounts profitability criteria. Thus it need not appear at all in the evaluation at the end of the period, if it is not likely to happen.

The analysis has shown that for the same cash flow the project with the higher working capital shows the better results in the books. Or conversely for the same results in the books in terms of NI/NCE in individual years, the project with the highest working capital shows the higher earning power.

However it is not only the nature of the investment which may cause discrepancies between the cash flow and the corresponding net income; nor the fact by itself that the realisation of working capital at the end of the period constitutes an integral part of the discipline of the discounted cash flow, whether the evaluator considers it a sound assumption or not. Discrepancies can also be caused by an early realisation of working capital because it is confidently expected, coupled with a relationship between cash generation and depreciation which produces book losses. Early realisation of working capital, i.e., before the last year in which a cash flow is generated adds to an early timing of the cash flow, and thus assists in raising the earning power; whilst a positive cash flow whether associated with book losses or not, has the same effect. The net result may be for a satisfactory earning power to hide unsatisfactory results in accounting terms. Project 4.3 from the actual experience of the author illustrates such a case (see Table 4.6). In spite of a satisfactory earning power of 13.3% (life time 11 years of which 10 operating years), it shows book losses in 5 years out of 10. Details are as follows:

A commercial life time of 5 years was foreseen for a project which is to manufacture a raw material for further processing. However some sales to third parties were anticipated in years 3 and 4, and debtors were expected to be associated with them in the same years. It was anticipated that these debtors would be liquidated in year 5 when

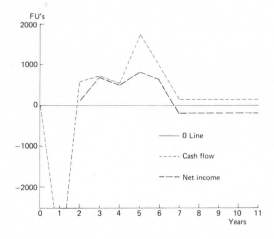

Graph 4.5. A comparison of the time profile of the cash flow and net income of project 4.3.

TABLE 4.6
The cash flow, net income, net capital employed and NI/NCE of project 4.3 (in FU's).

Year	CBT	Tax	Cash generation	Capital expenditure	Debtors	Cash flow	
1				3300		(3300)	
2	613	54	559			559	
3	1535	478	1057		(319)	738	EP:
4	1278	436	842		(281)	561	13.3%
5	1810	681	1129		600	1729	
6	1484	531	953			953	
7		(152)	152			152	
8		(152)	152			152	
9		(152)	152			152	
10		(152)	152			152	
11		(152)	152			152	

Year	Cash generation	Depreciation 10%	Net income
1			
2	559	330	229
3	1057	330	727
4	842	330	512
5	1129	330	799
6	953	330	623
7	152	330	(178)
8	152	330	(178)
9	152	330	(178)
10	152	330	(178)
11	152	330	(178)

Year	Book value	Debtors	NCE	NI/NCE
1	3,300		3,300	
2	2,970		2,970	7.7
3	2,640	319	2,959	24.6
4	2,310	600	2,910	17.6
5	1,980		1,980	40.4
6	1,650		1,650	37.8
7	1,320		1,320	neg.
8	990		990	neg.
9	660		660	neg.
10	330		330	neg.
11	0		0	neg.

sales terminate. After year 6 the plant has to be depreciated for another 5 years because fiscal laws do not allow a lump sum depreciation in year 6. As the plant forms part of the existing complex, any depreciation losses can be subtracted from the fiscal profits of the complex as a whole, resulting in tax savings. This can be treated as a positive cash flow because the savings are directly associated with the new project. Thus there is a positive cash flow in each of the years 7–11, but also a book loss, as a result of the depreciation of the plant being continued after year 6. In spite of a satisfactory earning power of over 13% in a 10-year operating life time, there are book losses for 5 years. The relationship through time of net income and the corresponding cash flow is illustrated in Graph 4.5. It should be noted that a book loss does not necessarily mean a negative cash flow.

A further case in which such a situation may arise is illustrated by project 4.4 (see Table 4.7). Whilst it is fictitious, it has been inspired by an actual case known to the author. The figures have been slightly exaggerated in order to demonstrate the principles. In spite of a satisfactory earning power of 11.1% over an 11 year life time (10 operating years) the project shows a nil profit during the first 4 years of operations. This is caused again by a relatively low cash generation in the early years as compared with the depreciation. The attractive earning power is produced in spite of a relatively low cash flow in the early years as compared with the later years. A situation like this may be caused by a combination of the following factors: a slow sales build-up, a comparatively high level of fixed costs, and a large build up of working capital in the early years. Graph 4.6 illustrates the relationship through time of the cash flow and net income.

A third and last example which demonstrates that earning power may conceal in one figure situations which are unsatisfactory to the company in accounting terms, is provided by project 4.5 from the actual experience of the author (see Tables 4.8 and 4.9). The project shows an earning power of 12.2% with a life time of 22 years. On the face of it this appears to be satisfactory. Yet it conceals a book loss in years 2, 3 and 4 a negligible profit in year 5 (see Table 4.8) and an unsatisfactory NI/NCE in years 6 and 7 (see Table 4.9). The unsatisfactory profitability position in accounting terms is concealed in the

TABLE 4.7

A comparison of the net income and cash flow of project 4.4 (in FU's).

Year	Cash gen.	Capital exp.	Cash flow	Cash gen.	Dep.	Net income
1		1000	(1000)			
2	100		100	100	100	0
3	100		100	100	100	0
4	100		100	100	100	0
5	100		100	100	100	0
6	250		250	250	100	150
7	250		250	250	100	150
8	250		250	250	100	150
9	250		250	250	100	150
10	250		250	250	100	150
11	250		250	250	100	150
	EP (%): 11.1					

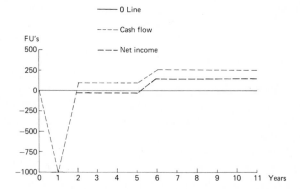

Graph 4.6. A comparison of the time profile of the cash flow and net income of project 4.4.

earning power by a long life time of 22 years (20 operating years) because the earning power is higher, the longer is the life time. (For an analysis of this see Chapter 2.) The true profitability in accounting terms would only be reflected in a lower earning power if a shorter life time is assumed (see Table 4.8). The conclusion is again reached that earning power is meaningless without specifying the life time. It all goes to show again, that a mere figure for earning power conceals in cases like these too much information which is vital to the management of the company. The figure of 12% in a 22 year life time certainly indicates that the profitability will be good in later years, which it is, but it is little use being prosperous in the long run if you go bankrupt in the short run.

Summarising the analysis of this chapter, and commenting on its findings, the discounted cash flow in its pure form forces the evaluator to assume that at the end of the life time of the project, all working capital is cashed in, whether he believes it or not. He is free to introduce other assumptions, but in expressing the results of the evaluation he would have to use besides earning power and PDV, further criteria which are extraneous to them. If he uses the discounted cash flow he cannot assume that no working capital will be cashed in, without there being a loss on the profit and loss account. Furthermore the discipline of the discounted cash flow forces the evaluator to make one more assumption in his evaluation which he does not need to make if he uses the financial accounts profitability criteria, i.e., on the life time of the project, because in the latter criteria the cashing in of working capital does not play an integral role in the computation. The assumption on life time is very important because earning power is sensitive to it, and no two earning powers are comparable unless the assumed life time is the same. If the evaluator uses the financial accounts profitability criteria, life time need only be introduced if it is essential and a reasonable estimate can be made. The evaluator is free to evaluate any number of years for which he thinks the future estimates have any meaning. This period is entirely unrelated to the life of the project. If it is shorter and no estimates have been made for the intervening years, he would have to stipulate in his evaluation that the investment is viable until it has reached its undefined or unknown commercial/technical end. The importance of evaluating the later years is discussed in Chapter 6.

It is often argued that the great advantage of a cash flow calculation is, that no book entries for depreciation are needed for it. This is quite

TABLE 4.8
The cash flow, net income and earning power of project 4.5 (in FU's).

Year	Cash gen.	Cap. exp.	Debtors	Other work. cap.	Cash flow	Cash gen.	Dep.	Stock evaluation	Net income
1		(2,400)			(2,400)				
2	(48)	(4,700)		(200)	(4,948)	(48)			(48)
3	202	(900)	(320)		(1,018)	202	(800)	386	(212)
4	650		(116)		534	650	(800)	58	(92)
5	844		(113)		731	844	(800)	26	70
6	1,014		(111)		903	1,014	(800)	29	243
7	1,176		(109)		1,067	1,176	(800)	32	408
8	1,347		(108)		1,239	1,347	(800)	20	567
9	1,484		(90)		1,394	1,484	(800)	29	713
10	1,625		(94)		1,531	1,625	(800)	36	861
11	1,833		(109)		1,724	1,833	(800)	(9)	1,024
12	1,869		(22)		1,847	1,869	(800)	(4)	1,065
13	1,867				1,867	1,867			1,867
14	1,867				1,867	1,867			1,867
15	1,867				1,867	1,867			1,867
16	1,867				1,867	1,867			1,867
17	1,867				1,867	1,867			1,867
18	1,867				1,867	1,867			1,867
19	1,607				1,607	1,607			1,607
20	1,607				1,607	1,607			1,607
21	1,607				1,607	1,607			1,607
22	1,607				1,607	1,607			1,607
Res. value					1,995				
Total					22,229				22,229

Life time (years)		EP (%)	
12		6	
17		11	
22		12	

true – except of course for the tax calculation – but it should be added that this advantage is replaced by two much greater disadvantages, i.e., that it *commits* the evaluator to make an assumption on working capital which may be at variance with his own expectations; and that

TABLE 4.9
The net capital employed and NI/NCE of project 4.5 (in FU's).

Year	Capital at cost	Deprecia-tion(cum.)	Book value	Stocks	Debtors	Other work. cap.	Losses	Net cap. empl.	NI/NCE (%)
1	2,400		2,400					2,400	–
2	7,100		7,100			200	48	7,348	(0.7)
3	8,000	(800)	7,200	386	320	200	260	8,366	(2.5)
4	8,000	(1,600)	6,400	444	436	200	352	7,832	(1.2)
5	8,000	(2,400)	5,600	470	549	200	282	7,101	1.0
6	8,000	(3,200)	4,800	499	660	200	39	6,198	3.9
7	8,000	(4,000)	4,000	531	769	200		5,500	7.4
8	8,000	(4,800)	3,200	551	877	200		4,828	11.7
9	8,000	(5,600)	2,400	580	967	200		4,147	17.2
10	8,000	(6,400)	1,600	616	1,061	200		3,477	24.8
11	8,000	(7,200)	800	607	1,170	200		2,777	36.9
12	8,000	(8,000)	–	603	1,192	200		1,995	53.4
13	8,000	(8,000)	–	603	1,192	200		1,995	93.5
14	8,000	(8,000)	–	603	1,192	200		1,995	93.5
15	8,000	(8,000)	–	603	1,192	200		1,995	93.5
16	8,000	(8,000)	–	603	1,192	200		1,995	93.5
17	8,000	(8,000)	–	603	1,192	200		1,995	93.5
18	8,000	(8,000)	–	603	1,192	200		1,995	93.5
19	8,000	(8,000)	–	603	1,192	200		1,995	80.5
20	8,000	(8,000)	–	603	1,192	200		1,995	80.5
21	8,000	(8,000)	–	603	1,192	200		1,995	80.5
22	8,000	(8,000)	–	603	1,192	200		1,995	80.5

it *commits* him to make an estimate of the life time of the project which it is not essential for him to make because an alternative financial method is available which does not require it.

Many situations may arise in which earning power is not a reliable guide to the profitability position as shown in the books of the company. The cause of this is, that the profitability criteria of the discounted cash flow and those of the financial accounts treat fixed investment and working capital very differently. A given cash flow with a given earning power shows very different results in the books of the company according to whether the proportion of fixed investment to working capital is high or low. Everything else being equal the results in terms of NI/NCE during the early years of the operation of the investment are higher and those in the later years are lower, the higher the proportion of working capital to fixed investment. Conversely with a given NI/NCE in each individual year, the earning power is higher, the higher is the proportion of working capital to fixed investment.

Of no less importance in causing situations in which earning power may not be a reliable guide to the net income and profitability position, are sustained runs of book losses associated with positive cash flows; or combinations of a slow sales build-up, a high level of fixed costs and a large build-up of working capital in the early years; or a very long life time of the project, and the reader may well be acquainted with many others. Thus a given earning power does not represent a unique result in the books of the company because it generates different results according to the relative value of the basic parameters. Cases like the ones studied may well be rare, but rather than be right most of the time it is far better to be right all the time, which it is possible to be. One cannot escape the conclusion that earning power conceals too much vital information in one figure. So indeed does the weighted average of the NI/NCE over the whole period, except that earning power derives its meaning from summarising a number of years, whereas NI/NCE has a meaning for individual years. Therefore NI/NCE can be separately specified for individual years according to the needs of the situation.

Thus the technique of recording the results of the company's operations by accounting methods differs far too much from that of the cash flow method, to ignore the difference altogether. Discounted cash flow does not instil the right discipline on those who have to think about the future of the company because it does not make the reporting system on project evaluation conform to the true aims of the company, i.e., to achieve a sound net income, and a sound profitability in accounting terms. It lacks impact because averages or summarises of averages may conceal figures in individual years, which may be of vital interest to the survival of the company. Therefore it may also be vague. Discounted cash flow carries the image of being a superior technique in that it is an automatic tool which makes it unnecessary for the management to apply further judgment. It implies that the profitability should only be compared with the 'cost of capital' – over an unspecified period.[5] It may therefore be misleading. The criteria of the discounted cash flow do not show how the summary was arrived at, nor as later chapters will show,[6] the profitability in the short run or in the long run, or the place of the profitability within the growth process of the company.

[5] See Chapter 2.
[6] See Chapters 6 and 7.

CHAPTER 5

PRESENT DAY VALUE AS A SELECTION CRITERION FOR MUTUALLY EXCLUSIVE PROJECTS

In the procedure of the discounted cash flow, the profitability of a project is summed up by discounting the cash flow at a discount rate higher or lower than the earning power, so as to obtain the positive or negative present day value at that discount rate – the PDV criterion. If this is done for two or more projects between which a choice has to be made, then only the amounts of the PDV's at that discount rate are compared; and the highest PDV points automatically to the preferred alternative. Unlike the financial accounts profitability criteria in which separate parameters such as net income, net capital employed and net income as a percentage of net capital employed have to be handled, PDV summarises profitability in one figure. For that reason it is very convenient (see also Chapter 2) and suits useful disciplines as that of, e.g., a decision tree.

However the relationship between the size of the PDV, and the timing of the cash flow[7] may seriously affect the soundness of the method – and thus the consequent assessment – and lead to wrong conclusions in cases which by their very nature imply a choice between an early and a late cash flow. Two examples in which this may occur (and in fact has occurred) are:

(1) where a choice has to be made between manufacturing a product or buying it in; and
(2) where a decision has to be made on the capacity of a plant.

These problems will be further explored in this chapter.

[7]See Chapter 3.

If a manager faces the alternatives between manufacturing a product and buying it in, he really has to decide between:

Alternative 1

Incurring costs in the early period (such as investment in manufacturing plant, pre-operational expenses associated with it, running the plant below full capacity in the initial year(s), etc.), and in compensation reap the benefit of a possibly attractive manufacturing profit and NI/NCE in the later years.

Alternative 2

Invest a far smaller sum of money (e.g., for storing and handling the product) without the benefit of a possibly attractive manufacturing profit in later years.

The details of such a problem, which has been taken from the actual experience of the author, are given in Tables 5.1 and 5.2. Two alternatives have been worked out: project 5.1 (own manufacture) for manufacturing the product, and project 5.2 (purchase) for buying it in. Either of the two alternatives is considered to be essential for the continuation of the business. They are therefore mutually exclusive.

The object of the computation is to calculate differentials for the cash flow, net income and net capital employed. In the two cases a value for the product has been put in at a 'netback' of FU 9.5/ton. Although this does not represent an actual cash in-flow component, it is convenient because it avoids too many negative figures in the cash flow computations. Of course the differentials would have been identical if these netbacks had been left out in either alternative.

The project is to form part of a large existing complex, justifying the assumption that any taxable losses give rise to a tax credit.

In alternative 1, project 5.1 (own manufacture), a capital outlay of FU 124.0 is foreseen (see Table 5.1) a heavy investment as compared with the incoming cash flow in the following 5 years of the operation of the project. There is a positive margin between netbacks and costs

– on which taxes have to be paid (the following year). In the last (residual) year 8 when the project is terminated the undepreciated part of the plant is wholly depreciated, giving rise to a tax credit of FU 10.4. In the same year working capital is cashed in at a price equal to its historic valuation of FU 43.7, giving rise to neither profit nor loss in that year. The total residual value is FU 54.1.

In alternative 2, project 5.2 (purchase), an investment of only FU 34.1 is foreseen (see Table 5.2). The product is bought at a price of £ 9.5/ton, the market value, and it leaves no margin as compared with the value of the product when it is manufactured. The positive cash flow arises entirely from the fact that there is a tax credit due to depreciation of the investment. The stock of product which has to be maintained on the site, is entirely financed by the supplier, i.e., working capital is equal to creditors. On balance there is therefore no residual value for working capital at the end of the period (year 8). In the same year the remaining undepreciated part of the investment is fully depreciated giving rise to a tax credit of FU 8.3.

A comparison of the two cash flows shows that the total of the cash flow over the whole period for project 5.1 (own manufacture) is FU 30.6, whilst that of project 5.2 (purchase) is minus FU 18.7 – see also Graph 5.1. The cash flow profile of 'own manufacture' shows a very much steeper upward incline (from a low of minus FU 109.7 in year 2 to a high of plus FU 54.1 in year 8) than that of 'purchase', which increases from minus FU 34.1 in year 2 to FU 9.3 in year 4 and FU 8.3 in year 8.

In the light of the structure in time of these cash flows, it is not surprising that their relative PDV's at various discount rates do not provide a clear cut indication of what the preferred choice should be (see Graph 5.1). The undiscounted PDV of project 5.1 (own manufacture) at FU 30.6 is far higher than that of the negative FU 18.7 of project 5.2 (purchase). Yet the 10% PDV of project 5.2 (purchase) is higher than that of project 5.1 (own manufacture), and so is the 12% PDV. At a discount rate of 9% the PDV's of the two alternatives are equal. At a discount rate higher than 9% the PDV of project 5.2 (purchase) is higher than that of the alternative, and at a discount rate lower than 9% the reverse is true.

TABLE 5.1

The cash flow, PDV, net income, net capital employed and payout time of project 5.1 (own manufacture) (in FU's).

	1	2	3	4	5	6	7	8	Total
Sales (tons/annum)									
(1) Sales			25,000	35,000	35,000	35,000	35,000	35,000	
(2) Stocks			5,845						
(3) Production			30,845	35,000	35,000	35,000	35,000	35,000	
Cash flow									
(4) Netback @ FU 9.5/ton			237.5	332.5	332.5	332.5	332.5		
(5) Fixed plus variable costs (excluding for stocks)			231.6	289.1	289.1	289.1	289.1		
(6) Cash before tax			5.9	43.4	43.4	43.4	43.4		179.5
(7) Fiscal depreciation			(19.0)	(15.0)	(12.8)	(10.9)	(9.3)	(57.0)	(124.0)
(8) Taxable			(13.1)	28.4	30.6	32.5	34.1	(57.0)	55.5
(9) Tax 45%				5.9	(12.8)	(13.8)	(14.6)	10.4	(24.9)
(10) Cash generation			5.9	49.3	30.6	29.6	28.8	10.4	154.6
(11) Capital expenditure	(20.0)	(104.0)							(124.0)
(12) Other working capital		(5.7)							(5.7)
(13) Stocks			(38.0)						(38.0)
(14) Residual value working capital								43.7	43.7
(15) Cash flow	(20.0)	(109.7)	(32.1)	49.3	30.6	29.6	28.8	54.1	30.6

Net income

(16) Cash before tax			5.9	43.4	43.4	43.4	43.4		179.5
(17) Depreciation			(12.4)	(12.4)	(12.4)	(12.4)	(12.4)	(62.0)	(124.0)
(18) Tax			5.9	(12.8)	(13.8)	(14.6)	(15.3)	25.7	(24.9)
(19) Net income			(0.6)	18.2	17.2	16.4	15.7	(36.3)	30.6

Net capital employed

(20) Book value	20.0	124.0	111.6	99.2	86.8	74.4	62.0	0	
(21) Working capital		5.7	43.7	43.7	43.7	43.7	43.7	0	
(22) NCE	20.0	129.7	155.3	142.9	130.5	118.1	105.7	0	

Present day value

Discount rate (%)	6	(7.6)
	8	(16.3)
	10	(23.5)
	12	(29.6)

POT (years) 7.4

EP (%) 4.5

TABLE 5.2

The cash flow, PDV, net income, net capital employed and pay-out time of project 5.2 (purchase) (in FU's).

	1	2	3	4	5	6	7	8	Total
Sales (tons/annum)									
(1) Sales			25,000	35,000	35,000	35,000	35,000		
(2) Stocks			5,845						
(3) Production			30,845	35,000	35,000	35,000	35,000		
Cash flow									
(4) Netback @ FU 9.5/ton			237.5	332.5	332.5	332.5	332.5		
(5) Costs (excluding stocks) @ FU 9.5/ton			237.5	332.5	332.5	332.5	332.5		
(6) Cash before tax			0	0	0	0	0		
(7) Fiscal depreciation			(5.2)	(4.1)	(3.5)	(3.0)	(2.6)	(15.7)	(34.1)
(8) Taxable			(5.2)	(4.1)	(3.5)	(3.0)	(2.6)	(15.7)	(34.1)
(9) Tax 45%				2.3	1.8	1.6	1.4	8.3	15.4
(10) Cash generation			0	2.3	1.8	1.6	1.4	8.3	15.4
(11) Capital expenditure		(34.1)							(34.1)
(12) Creditors			46.0	7.0					53.0
(13) Stocks			(53.0)						(53.0)
(14) Residual value working capital								0	
(15) Cash flow		(34.1)	(7.0)	9.3	1.8	1.6	1.4	8.3	(18.7)

Net income

(16) Cash before tax		0	0	0	0	0	0	0
(17) Depreciation		(3.4)	(3.4)	(3.4)	(3.4)	(3.4)	(17.1)	(34.1)
(18) Tax		2.3	1.8	1.6	1.4	1.2	7.1	15.4
(19) Net income		(1.1)	(1.6)	(1.8)	(2.0)	(2.2)	(10.0)	(18.7)

Net capital employed

(20) Book value	34.1	30.7	27.3	23.9	20.5	17.1	0	
(21) Working capital		7.0	0	0	0	0	0	
(22) NCE	34.1	37.7	27.3	23.9	20.5	17.1	0	

Present day value

Discount rate (%)		
	6	(20.3)
	8	(20.4)
	10	(20.5)
	12	(20.5)

POT (years) > 8

EP (%)   negative

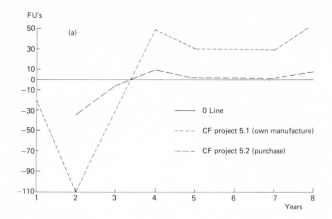

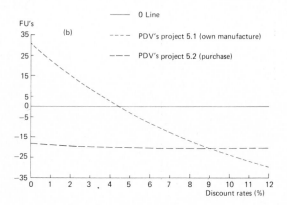

Graph 5.1. (a) A comparison of the cash flows of project 5.1 (own manufacture) and project 5.2 (purchase). (b) A comparison of the PDV's at various discount rates of project 5.1 (own manufacture) and project 5.2 (purchase).

The position is in fact that of Case 5 in Chapter 3 whereby project 5.1 (own manufacture) has the early cash flow and project 5.2 (purchase) has the late cash flow. Thus:

project 5.1 project 5.2
PDV 0%: ECF > LCF

project 5.1 project 5.2
EP: ECF > LCF

Therefore at discount rates lower than the earning power of the differential cash flow – in this case 9% – the PDV's of project 5.1 (own manufacture) are higher and at discount rates higher than the earning power of the differential cash flow those of project 5.2 (purchase) are higher.

If a choice were to be made solely on the basis of PDV, then the discount rate would determine the preferred choice. If it is accepted that the choice of the discount rate is fairly arbitrary, and that in any case it leaves a fair margin of choice between reasonable limits, then this problem is a clear illustration of the fact that PDV may be of no assistance in suggesting the preferred course of action. In fact it clouds a true definition of the problem, because it relegates into the background the alternatives between which the management has to choose: investing money and reaping the manufacturing profit, or investing no money and making a small book loss.

Clearly the financial accounts profitability criteria must again be resorted to, because they must be the ultimate judge. On that evidence there is a strong case for project 5.1 (own manufacture) to be the preferred choice. The higher net income of project 5.1 (own manufacture) arises from the fact that there is a positive margin between the market value of the product, and the cost at which the company can manufacture the product. This margin is not available to the company in project 5.2 (purchase) because in that case, it is paid out to the supplier. As against this, more capital has to be invested in the case of project 5.1 (own manufacture). Thus the financial resources available to the company will be of much importance in determining the choice. This consideration, and no doubt many others which cannot easily be quantified play their part in the decision, but a detailed examination of those factors would be outside the scope of this study. In any event the example goes to show that more information than just the PDV's of the two cash flows is essential as a basis for a decision. It is not suggested that cases of this kind occur very frequently. Indeed they are rare. Nevertheless they are worth studying because they are of assistance in deepening the understanding of the PDV principle.

A further problem in which a choice between an early and a late cash flow is of importance, is that of selecting a capacity of a plant. The case discussed is again from actual experience.

A plant to produce a product *Y* could be built at a capacity of either 33,000 or 40,000 tons per annum – respectively called project 5.3 (33,000 t/a) and project 5.4 (40,000 t/a). For short these alternatives will be referred to as alt. 33,000 and alt. 40,000.

The plant was not to form part of an existing complex. It was an entirely new enterprise for which a new company had to be incorporated. Taxes would therefore be payable as soon as the taxable net income is cumulatively positive.

The larger plant involves a greater capital outlay (see Table 5.3). As against this its cash flow is higher at full capacity than that of the smaller plant. The larger plant reaches full capacity at a later stage after it has gone into operation, than the smaller one. The situation can be summed up by saying that the cash flow of alt. 40,000 is later than that of alt. 33,000.

At discount rates lower than the earning power of the differential cash flow – which in this case is 13.8% – the PDV's of alt. 40,000 are higher than those of alt. 33,000, and at discount rates higher than the earning power of the differential cash flow they are lower (see Graph 5.2). The situation is in fact that of Case 6 of Chapter 3 whereby alt. 33,000 has the early cash flow and alt. 40,000 has the late cash flow:

	alt. 33,000	alt. 40,000
PDV 0%:	ECF <	LCF

	alt. 33,000	alt. 40,000
EP:	ECF >	LCF

Whilst the earning power of alt. 40,000 is very slightly lower than

TABLE 5.3
A comparison of the cash flows, earning power, PDV's and pay-out time of alt.
40,000 and alt. 33,000 (in Fu's).

Year	Cash flows			
	Alternative		Differential	Differential (cum.)
	40,000	33,000		
1	(766)	(714)	(52)	(52)
2	(2,496)	(2,288)	(208)	(260)
3	(4,586)	(4,151)	(435)	(695)
4	(502)	(391)	(111)	(806)
5	1,687	1,713	(26)	(832)
6	2,050	2,076	(26)	(858)
7	2,240	2,163	77	(781)
8	2,137	2,078	59	(722)
9	2,220	2,041	179	(543)
10	2,467	2,041	426	(117)
11	2,533	2,041	492	375
12	2,533	2,041	492	867
13	2,533	2,041	492	1,359
RV	2,069	1,760	309	1,668
Total	14,119	12,451	1,668	

	Alternative		Differential
	40,000	33,000	
EP (%)	16.2	16.5	13.8
PDV (%) 10	2,673	2,465	208
12	1,591	1,508	83
14	742	752	(10)
16	46	131	(85)
POT (years)	8.1	7.8	10.2

that of alt. 33,000, the larger plant yields a differential earning power
of 13.8% notwithstanding the fact that the differential cash flow is

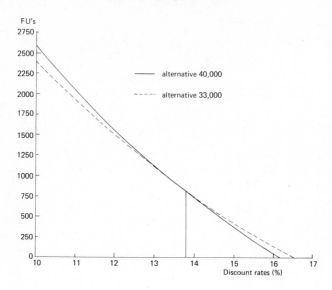

Graph 5.2. A comparison of the PDV's at various discount rates of alternative 40,000
and alternative 33,000.

negative in the first 6 years, small in the next 2, and only of any significance in the last 5 years of operation (see Table 5.3).

A discount rate of the order of 14% was considered appropriate at
the time because there were considerable risks involved in the project.
The preferred choice by the criteria of earning power and PDV is:

	Preferred choice
Earning power	alt. 40,000
PDV (discount rate smaller than 13.8%)	alt. 40,000
PDV (discount rate higher than 13.8%)	alt. 33,000
Pay-out time	alt. 33,000

Again this represents insufficient basis for a decision. The choice of the discount rate contains in itself a considerable element of arbitrariness. There are no really logical grounds for rejecting any figure between say 12% and 15%. Yet the precise level is vital for the decision.

Furthermore the residual value and particularly the differential of the residual value, is large in comparison with the respective cash flows notwithstanding the fact that cashing in of the working capital after 10 operating years was considered to be most unlikely. There is therefore a corresponding distortion in the profitability profile as compared with that of net income/net capital employed.

The pay-out time of the additional capital outlay of the bigger plant is very long (10.2 years). By that criterion selection of the smaller plant would tend to be a better choice.

Taking all factors into account, further analysis in terms of net income and net income/net capital employed is needed.

The larger capacity causes a differential loss during 4 years out of the first 5 years of operation (see Table 5.4). In year 7 the larger plant shows a differential surplus of FU 134.0. It is comparatively small as compared with that of the later years and arises as a result of the tax situation. The cumulative differential net income does not become positive until year 10 – the seventh year of operation of the plant.

The differential NI/NCE (see Graph 5.3) is negative in one pre-operational year (year 3) and in 4 years out of the first 5 years of operation. If the overall profitability as aimed at by the company is 12% NI/NCE then the company has to wait 7 years after the first capital has been spent on the building of the plant, until that level is reached on the marginal net capital employed which arises from building the bigger plant. Even then it is negative again in the following year (year 8) and only thereafter is the differential NI/NCE on the bigger investment satisfactory. Cumulatively and taking into account the fact that there is NCE in years 1, 2, and 3 against which there is no NI – the differential NI/NCE does not become positive until year 10, the 7th year of operation. Thus on the evidence of the financial account profitability criteria the smaller plant would seem to be preferable. This is in contradiction to the solution offered by a 10% or 12% PDV.

TABLE 5.4

A comparison of the net income, differential net income, cumulative differential net income, NI/NCE, differential NI/NCE and cumulative differential NI/NCE of alternatives 40,000 and 33,000 (Table A in FU's, Table B in %).

Year	(A) Net income				(B) NI/NCE			
	Alternative		Diff.	Diff. (cum.)	Alternative		Diff.	Diff. (cum.)
	40,000	30,000			40,000	30,000		
1					nil	nil	nil	nil
2					nil	nil	nil	nil
3	(896)	(803)	(93)	(93)	neg.	neg.	neg.	neg.
4	666	754	(88)	(181)	8.0	10.0	neg.	neg.
5	1,179	1,262	(83)	(264)	15.5	17.9	neg.	neg.
6	1,537	1,620	(83)	(347)	21.7	24.6	neg.	neg.
7	1,577	1,443	134	(213)	24.5	24.6	17.1	neg.
8	1,379	1,437	(58)	(271)	24.3	27.5	neg.	neg.
9	1,668	1,436	232	(39)	32.5	31.1	42.6	neg.
10	1,874	1,436	438	399	41.4	35.8	85.2	6.6
11	1,871	1,436	435	834	48.4	42.1	95.1	12.8
12	1,871	1,436	435	1,269	58.4	51.2	108.7	18.3
13	1,871	1,436	435	1,704	73.5	65.2	126.8	23.5
RV	(478)	(442)	(36)	1,668	–	–	–	–
Total	14,119	12,451	1,668					

In spite of the foregoing it may still be argued that although selection by the PDV criterion may result in the alternative with the later cash flow being selected, it would be the desirable choice between them because it would mean that the alternative with the highest total undiscounted cash flow (and highest net income) during the lifetime of the project, is selected. This is true, provided it is really believed that the higher cash flow in the later years will in fact be realised. There are two reasons why doubts may be cast on this possibility:

(1) There is in any case a higher degree of uncertainty attached to estimates relating to an even remoter and therefore even more nebulous future.

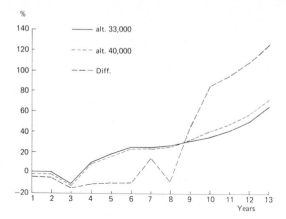

Graph 5.3. A comparison of tne NI/NCE and differential NI/NCE through time of alternative 33,000 and alternative 40,000.

(2) In cases in which a relatively low cash flow in the early years and a higher one in the later years may be caused by a greater capacity, a need may be felt by the industry to achieve a quick loading to full capacity, and this may cause a downward pressure on prices and thus on cash flows.

Thus the very validity of the estimates of the high cash flow in later years may be open to doubt. If, nevertheless, the PDV principle is used blindly as a selection criterion, then the possible disadvantage of a longer pay-out time and a lower profitability in terms of cash flow or NI/NCE in the early years, may not be compensated by a higher profitability in later years. The investor would then have the worst of two possible worlds. It clearly shows that the PDV criterion may contradict the principle of earning power because the latter emphasises an early cash flow and quick results.

Taking the problem of varying the earning power and/or PDV by varying the capacity of the plant, one step further, it may then be asked what the optimum earning power and/or PDV should be for any one proposed investment. There is no inherent reason in the theory of the discounted cash flow why either earning power or present day value should not be optimised – or in the language of the theory – why the capacity of the plant should not be fixed at a level where the marginal earning power is equal to the assumed cost of capital, or where the PDV at a discount rate equal to the assumed cost of capital is optimised – the two criteria lead to the same optimum capacity. Indeed, the determination of this optimum would take the theory of the discounted cash flow to its logical conclusion. It would also be appropriate to investigate what basic data match this optimum, and then to confront those basic data with judgment.

The profitability of any planned investment can be varied by choosing alternative capacities, because it is possible to vary the structure of the cash flow by varying the capacity. As has been pointed out before, the underlying principle is that a plant with a small capacity will have a smaller negative cash flow associated with it in the early years than a plant with a large capacity. Also its off-take will be constrained at full capacity at a lower level and at an earlier moment; thus its positive cash flow in later years will level off at a lower level, and at an earlier point in time, than that of a large plant. However the implications of these principles for the profitability over a full range of capacities can only be studied in more detail if the basic data associated with those capacities are determined first. The case is again from the actual experience of the author. However slight modifications have been made so as to illustrate the principles.

It is assumed that the volume of demand for the end product of project 5.3 is 150,000 tons in year 2, and that it increases at an annual growth rate of 4% in the following years. The volume of demand would thus develop as follows:

Year 2	150,000	
Year 3	156,000	Growth rate 4%
Year 4	162,200	
Year 5	168,700	
etc.		

The cost of plants with capacities of:

150,000	tons/annum
155,000	tons/annum
160,000	tons/annum
165,000	tons/annum etc.

up to and including 220,000 tons/annum were then calculated by applying the following formula:

Cost of plant with capacity $x =$

$$C_x = \text{FU } 5{,}000{,}000 \times \left(\frac{x}{100{,}000} \right)^{0.65}.$$

This implies that a plant with a capacity of 100,000 tons/annum costs FU 5,000,000.

Labour costs were calculated by using a similar formula:

Labour costs of plant with a capacity $x =$

$$L_x = \text{FU } 100{,}000 \times \left(\frac{x}{100{,}000} \right)^{0.15}.$$

Other basic data associated with these plant capacities are listed in Table 5.5. They are consistent with the above formulas.

Cash flows for each capacity were then calculated. A detailed example for a plant with a capacity of 185,000 tons/annum is given in Table 1.1 for project 'P'. Calculations for plants with capacities from 150,000 tons/annum to 220,000 tons/annum were made along identical lines. Project 'P', Table 1.1, belongs to the series.

Six of the resulting cash flows at these capacities are shown in Table 5.6. It should be noted that the year in which full capacity is reached does not necessarily coincide with the year in which the cash flow levels out, e.g., at a capacity of 160,000 tons/annum full capacity is reached in year 4, whereas the cash flow levels out at its maximum level in year 5. The difference is due to capacity taken up for stock build-up.

The time profile of the cash flows for capacities of 150,000 and 220,000 tons/annum is illustrated in Graph 5.4. It will be seen that the

TABLE 5.5

The basic data for the various plant capacities of project 5.3 .

	Units	Capacity (000's tons/annum)					
		150	160	175	190	205	220
1 Sales year 2	000's tons	←			150		→
2 Growth rate	%	←			4		→
3 Netback	FU/ton	←			28		→
4 Variable costs	FU/ton	←			12		→
5 Fixed costs	FU 000's	733.4	757.2	793.2	827.2	860.4	893.0
6 Pre-operational expenses	FU 000's	195.3	203.4	215.8	227.7	239.2	250.4
7 Phasing pre-operational expenses (% of total) year 2	%	←			40		→
8 year 3	%	←			60		→
9 Stock valuation (costs at full capacity including 10% depreciation)	FU/ton	21.2	21.0	20.6	20.3	20.1	19.9
10 Period of stocks	months	←			1		→
11 Depreciation	years	←			10		→
12 Tax	%	←			50		→
13 Capital expenditure	FU 000's	6510.0	6780.0	7194.0	7588.6	7972.8	8347.0
14 Phasing capital expenditure (% of total) year 1	%	←			40		→
15 2	%	←			40		→
16 3	%	←			20		→
17 Period of debtors	months	←			2		→
18 Other working capital	FU 000's	297.1	309.1	327.5	344.9	361.9	378.6
19 Residual value (= working capital)	FU 000's	1262.5	1335.1	1446.6	1555.0	1662.9	1770.4

TABLE 5.6

The cash flows of the various plant capacities of project 5.3 (in FU 000's).

Year	Capacity (000's tons/annum)					
	150	160	175	190	205	220
1	(2604.0)	(2712.0)	(2877.6)	(3035.4)	(3189.1)	(3338.8)
2	(2643.0)	(2752.7)	(2920.7)	(3080.9)	(3237.0)	(3388.9)
3	(1406.6)	(1460.0)	(1560.1)	(1655.3)	(1748.4)	(1839.3)
4	1158.8	1215.8	1224.5	1227.3	1230.0	1232.5
5	1158.8	1240.4	1272.9	1275.8	1278.4	1280.9
6	1158.8	1240.4	1323.3	1330.1	1332.8	1335.3
7	1158.8	1240.4	1363.1	1382.6	1385.2	1387.7
8	1158.8	1240.4	1363.1	1438.9	1443.6	1446.1
9	1158.8	1240.4	1363.1	1485.8	1500.8	1503.3
10	1158.8	1240.4	1363.1	1485.8	1561.6	1566.5
11	1158.8	1240.4	1363.1	1485.8	1608.4	1628.5
12	1158.8	1240.4	1363.1	1485.8	1608.4	1691.3
13	833.3	901.4	1003.4	1106.4	1209.8	1313.5
14	833.3	901.4	1003.4	1106.4	1209.8	1313.5
15	833.3	901.4	1003.4	1106.4	1209.8	1313.5
16	833.3	901.4	1003.4	1106.4	1209.8	1313.5
17	833.3	901.4	1003.4	1106.4	1209.8	1313.5
18	833.3	901.4	1003.4	1106.4	1209.8	1313.5
19	833.3	901.4	1003.4	1106.4	1209.8	1313.5
20	833.3	901.4	1003.4	1106.4	1209.8	1313.5
21	833.3	901.4	1003.4	1106.4	1209.8	1313.5
22	833.3	901.4	1003.4	1106.4	1209.8	1313.5
RV	1262.5	1335.1	1446.6	1555.0	1662.9	1770.4
Total	13,371	14,563	16,122	17,445	18,536	19,411

Year in which full capacity is reached:

| 3 | 4 | 6 | 8 | 10 | 12 |

cash flow of the larger plants starts at a lower level (higher investment) than that of the smaller plant. When the cash flow of the larger plant becomes positive it gradually slopes upwards to the level at which full capacity is reached. Even at partial capacity it is higher than that of the smaller plant. This is due to the fact that fixed costs per ton of the larger plant are lower than those of the smaller plant.

Although the earning powers of the cash flows remain approximately the same over a wide range of capacities (see Table 5.7), the dif-

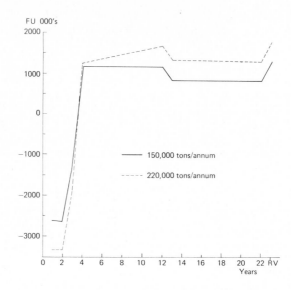

Graph 5.4. A comparison of the cash flow profiles of project 5.3 for capacities of
150,000 and 220,000 tons/annum.

ferential earning powers show a decline as capacity is increased from
23.7% at 155,000 tons/annum to 8.4% at 215,000 tons/annum.[8] Thus
taking the theory of the discounted cash flow to its logical conclusion
(and assuming a cost of capital of 8%), the profitability of the investment is optimised at a capacity of just over 215,000 tons/annum,
because at that capacity the marginal earning power is equal to the
cost of capital (see Graph 5.5). The PDV's at a discount rate of 8%
again show a maximum at a capacity of just over 215,000 tons/an-
num (see Graph 5.5), the same capacity at which the differential earning power of the stepwise increases in capacity is equal to 8%. This is
not unexpected because at the point at which the PDV curve at a dis-

[8] It has been necessary to take the earning powers and pay-out times to the third
decimal in order to illustrate the optimum. This is of course well within the margin of
error of the forecasts, but in this context it has been ignored in order to illustrate the
principles.

TABLE 5.7

The pay-out time, earning power, 8% PDV and the differential pay-out time and earning power of the various capacities of project 5.3.

Capacity (000's tons)	POT (years)	EP %	PDV 8% (FU 000's)	Increase in capacity (000's tons)	Diff. POT (years)	Diff. EP %
150	8.742	12.712	2,387.5			
155	8.652	12.951	2,577.0	150 → 155	6.088	23.727
160	8.603	13.112	2,731.4	155 → 160	7.159	19.193
165	8.579	13.226	2,865.9	160 → 165	7.866	17.263
170	8.576	13.285	2,983.7	165 → 170	8.489	15.781
175	8.595	13.326	3,083.7	170 → 175	9.215	14.447
180	8.634	13.328	3,164.0	175 → 180	9.922	13.091
185	8.689	13.300	3,235.0	180 → 185	10.577	12.536
190	8.752	13.268	3,297.8	185 → 190	10.968	12.000
195	8.835	13.198	3,336.7	190 → 195	11.968	10.480
200	8.920	13.119	3,366.8	195 → 200	12.576	9.909
205	9.002	13.042	3,394.8	200 → 205	12.954	9.820
210	9.082	12.951	3,405.7	205 → 210	13.997	8.726
215	9.161	12.862	3,411.1	210 → 215	14.441	8.381
220	9.243	12.697	3,401.4	215 → 220	15.366	7.393

count rate of 8% shows an optimum, the PDV's of two small successive steps in capacity increases are equal, and this occurs at the capacity at which the earning power of the differential cash flows is also equal to 8% (see Chapter 3). It is the point at which according to the theory of the discounted cash flow the investment is optimised.

It is of interest to study the various facets of this optimum in detail.

A plant with a capacity of 215,000 tons/annum does not reach full capacity until year 12, the tenth year of operation. Commonsense makes the evaluator suspect that this is financially unacceptable even in a technologically static society. The profitability in accounting terms amply confirms this suspicion (see Table 5.8). The NI/NCE does not reach a satisfactory level until year 7 or 8, i.e., until the 5th or 6th year of operation of the plant – the criterion for 'satisfactory' or 'unsatisfactory' in this context is again whether the profitability of the new investment is higher or lower than that of the company as a whole. If past balance sheets of the company have shown 14% NI/NCE, and if it is the objective of the management to maintain it,

H.P.J. Heukensfeldt Jansen

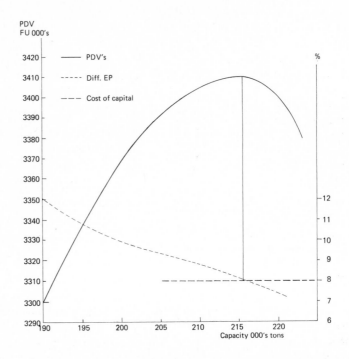

Graph 5.5. The PDV's and differential earning powers of the stepwise increases in capacity of project 5.3, and the optimum capacity at a cost of capital of 8%.

TABLE 5.8

The financial results in accounting terms of the optimum capacity of project 5.3 during the first 6 operating years (in %).

Year	Operating year	NI/NCE
3	1	4.2
4	2	5.6
5	3	6.9
6	4	8.6
7	5	10.8
8	6	13.7

then the new investment will be a burden to the company for 8 years from the moment the first capital is spent on the project. This is unacceptable. If the new investment were not part of an existing business, but if it were an entirely new enterprise incorporated in a new and independent company, it would be even more unacceptable – assuming at least that in the judgment of the management a 14% NI/NCE is the minimum profitability required to keep the company afloat in the long run.

However it is not contended that the application of the theory of the discounted cash flow leads automatically to too large a plant. It may well be that the basic data which are applied to any other project lead to results which are acceptable if they are confronted with judgment. The important point to bear in mind is, that the discounted cash flow does not set a limit either to the discount rate or to the life time of the project.

Nor is it always possible to establish an optimum at all. Although in the search for an optimum a wide range of capacities has been explored from 150,000 to 220,000 tons/annum it is possible to introduce a discount rate of say 3% or 6% which results in there being no optimum at all within that range (see Table 5.9). At discount rates of 3% and 6% the optimum is well beyond 220,000 tons/annum. At a 10% discount rate the optimum is at 205,000 tons/annum.

The optimum capacity obtained by the criterion of the discounted cash flow is higher at a given cost of capital, the higher is the curve of

TABLE 5.9

The present day value of the various capacities of project 5.3 at increasing rates of discount (in FU's).

Discount rate (%)	Capacity (000's tons)			
	175	190	205	220
0	16,122	17,445	18,536	19,411
3	9,236	9,962	10,509	10,901
6	5,004	5,374	5,606	5,726
8	3,084	3,298	3,395	3,401
10	1,653	1,754	1,756	1,685

the differential earning power (see Graph 5.5). This would apply if each of the stepwise increases in capacity become more profitable as compared with the previous step, e.g., if the exponential for calculating the capital expenditure is lowered from 0.65 to say 0.40 or if labour costs are reduced. Table 5.10 illustrates the principle. In case A steps 1 and 2 which represent 'increases in capacity' have an earning power of respectively 6% and 10%, and the differential earning power is 50%. In Case B the investment needed to obtain the increased capacity is lower than in Case A, whilst the positive cash flow is higher because of reduced labour costs. Consequently the earning power of steps 1 and 2, and that of the differential are higher in Case B than in Case A. This results in a larger capacity for the 'B' series and thus with a given growth in demand as assumed for project 5.3 full capacity is reached at a later date. For instance:

	Series A	Series B
Year in which new capacity is required	7	9

TABLE 5.10
An illustration of the principle of a higher differential earning power with increases in capacity (in FU's).

	Step 1	Step 2	Differential
Case A	(90)	(100)	(10)
	95	110	15
EP (%)	6	10	50
Case B	(89)	(98)	(9)
	97	111	14
EP (%)	9	13	56

This means that with the lower profitability of Series A the costlier solution in time results, because a new plant has to be built sooner. Further pre-operational expenses are associated with the new plant. Higher pre-operational expenses – higher per ton of product – would have to be incurred at more frequent intervals than if plants with larger capacities were built. The same applies to capital expenditure and a similar role is played by the cost of capital. Table 5.9 illustrates that the optimum capacity for project 5.3 would be 205,000 tons/annum at a cost of capital of 10% and 215,000 tons/annum at a cost of capital of 8%. Thus the cost per ton of end-product over a long period is higher as a result of the higher cost of capital. By recommending a smaller plant if the margin between proceeds and the various cost components is lower, the method of the discounted cash flow aggravates the consequences of lower profitability. Higher costs per ton of end-product over the given period, are the inevitable consequence of a smaller plant. These implications of the DCF procedure are at variance with commonsense and sound judgment.

It remains to study the interrelationship of the PDV's associated with the stepwise increases in capacity. The steps have in common that up to the point at which the optimum is reached, the PDV's of the bigger capacities are higher. Therefore the bigger capacities are preferred. However the reasons why they are preferred are not uniform in the range. In fact the relationship between the PDV's in each of the stepwise increases falls under 3 different cases as defined in Chapter 3 (see Table 3.10 and Table 5.11), i.e., cases 5, 8 and 6. This is explained by the fact that (see Graph 5.6):

(1) the pay-out time shows a minimum at 170,000 tons/annum;
(2) the 0% PDV shows a steady increase as capacity is increased; and
(3) the earning power shows a maximum at 180,000 tons/annum.

Stage 1. Capacity is increased from 150,000 to 170,000 tons/annum in 4 steps. In each of these a late cash flow is replaced by an early cash flow. The 0% PDV and earning power rise as capacity is increased.

Stage 2. Capacity is increased from 170,000 to 180,000 tons/annum in 2 steps. In each of these an early cash flow is replaced by a late cash flow. The 0% PDV and earning power rise as capacity is increased.

Stage 3. Capacity is increased from 180,000 to 215,000 tons/annum in 7 steps. In each of these an early cash flow is replaced by a late cash flow. The 0% PDV rises and earning power falls as capacity is increased.

H.P.J. Heukensfeldt Jansen

TABLE 5.11

The stepwise increases in the capacities of project 5.3 in terms of the cases defined in Chapter 3.

Step	Increase in capacity (000's tons)	0% PDV	EP	Case	Preference
1	150 → 155	ECF > LCF	ECF > LCF	5	early 155
2	155 → 160	ECF > LCF	ECF > LCF	5	early 160
3	160 → 165	ECF > LCF	ECF > LCF	5	early 165
4	165 → 170	ECF > LCF	ECF > LCF	5	early 170
5	170 → 175	ECF < LCF	ECF < LCF	8	late 175
6	175 → 180	ECF < LCF	ECF < LCF	8	late 180
7	180 → 185	ECF < LCF	ECF > LCF	6	late 185
8	185 → 190	ECF < LCF	ECF > LCF	6	late 190
9	190 → 195	ECF < LCF	ECF > LCF	6	late 195
10	195 → 200	ECF < LCF	ECF > LCF	6	late 200
11	200 → 205	ECF < LCF	ECF > LCF	6	late 205
12	205 → 210	ECF < LCF	ECF > LCF	6	late 210
13	210 → 215	ECF < LCF	ECF > LCF	6	late 215
14	215 → 220	ECF < LCF	ECF > LCF	6	Discount rate

	< 7.4%	> 7.4%
	late	early
	220	215

The analysis demonstrates that there is a need to examine each stepwise increase in terms of the major profitability criteria which are available, those of pay-out time, earning power and financial accounts. Incidentally it also shows again that within this context direct comparisons of pay-out times have a role to play in financial analysis. So do direct comparisons of the earning power of individual cash flows as opposed to the earning power of the differential cash flows. They all describe the route towards the optimum, and they are vital instruments in analysing how the PDV curve will run at a given discount rate, and where the optimum, if there is one, will be.

Thus as far as pay-out time is concerned a capacity of 170,000

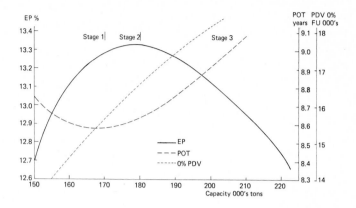

Graph 5.6. The earning power, pay-out time and 0% PDV of the various capacities of project 5.3.

tons/annum may be considered as the basis for a decision. It should be noted that the differential pay-out times increase as the capacity is increased (see Table 5.7). The criteria of the discounted cash flow suggest capacities of 180,000 and 215,000 tons/annum. The build-up towards the optimum demonstrates that even if earning power is used as a selection criterion (i.e., by using the differential procedure) a late cash flow may be preferred to an early cash flow, e.g., in the steps from 190,000 to 195,000 tons/annum or 200,000 to 205,000 tons/annum (see Chapter 3).

Anticipating on the suggestions in Chapter 7, the profitability in accounting terms during the first vital initial years, can be expressed as an average of the net income as a % of the net capital employed. This has been called the PIP and it is defined as the weighted average of the NI/NCE (expressed as a %) during the period which commences when the first capital on the project is spent and terminates in this case in the 5th year after the plant has come into operation.

The aggregate of the net income during that period shows an optimum at a capacity of 175,000 tons/annum (see Table 5.12 and Graph 5.7) whilst the sum total of the net capital employed over the first seven years shows a steady increase as the capacity increases (see

Graph 5.7). It is therefore obvious that the PIP shows a maximum, i.e., at 165,000 tons per annum (see Graph 5.8). This is interesting evidence as the basis for a decision, but again the differential PIP's of the stepwise increases is more important for selection purposes. In view of the fact that net income shows an optimum at 175,000 tons /annum it is not surprising that the differential PIP's become negative beyond that capacity (see Graph 5.8). On the evidence of the financial accounts criterion a capacity of 175,000 tons/annum could be considered. The optimum capacities which result by using the three different major criteria of profitability are summarised in Table 5.13.

It should be noted that none of the major criteria provide an objective function for establishing an optimum capacity. Pay-out time does not take into account any profitability after the pay-out period. If the discounted cash flow is used important estimates have to be made to which the solution is very sensitive, e.g., on the discount rate and the life time. If the PIP criterion is used, the (rather arbitrary) choice of the number of operating years is very vital, and again the criterion does not take into account any profitability after the PIP period. However the determination of an optimum by the discounted cash flow takes the theory to its logical conclusion. Rather than make a set of assumptions from which an optimum capacity follows – if it does – via essential assumptions on the cost of capital (discount rate), life time and operating years, it is far better to bring direct judgment to bear on the problem. Capacity should not follow from other data; it is a matter of direct judgment.

Summarising this experiment in establishing an optimum capacity, the PDV criterion pretends to give a direct answer to a solution because the optimum PDV should according to the theory optimise the investment. However it is possible to find examples from actual experience which by the very combination of the basic data result in unrealistic conclusions, e.g., a plant may be selected with too big a capacity, or there may not be an optimum at all. These situations may occur if the mutual relationships of the basic data exceed certain limits notwithstanding the fact that the theory of the discounted cash flow itself does not impose any limits upon its application.

Furthermore the arithmetical properties of the method result in the

TABLE 5.12

The total of the net income, net capital employed and their weighted average during the period from the first building years to the fifth operating year (inclusive) – the PIP – of the various capacities of project 5.3, and the differential PIP's of the stepwise increases in capacity.

Capacity (000's tons)	NI	NCE	PIP (%)	Capacity increase (000's tons)	Diff. PIP (%)
	(FU 000's)				
150	2,449	36,949	6.76	150 → 155	17.45
155	2,637	37,739	6.99	155 → 160	12.31
160	2,738	38,559	7.10	160 → 165	9.13
165	2,810	39,347	7.14	165 → 170	5.76
170	2,853	40,109	7.11	170 → 175	2.14
175	2,869	40,839	7.03	175 → 180	(2.90)
180	2,849	41,532	6.86	180 → 185	(6.60)
185	2,806	42,186	6.65	185 → 190	(9.98)
190	2,744	42,809	6.41	190 → 195	(10.00)
195	2,680	43,449	6.17	195 → 200	(9.93)
200	2,616	44,085	5.93	200 → 205	(10.12)
205	2,556	44,682	5.72	205 → 210	(9.82)
210	2,496	45,289	5.51	210 → 215	(9.95)
215	2,437	45,889	5.31	215 → 220	(10.04)
220					

size of certain cost components, e.g., pre-operational expenses, and capital expenditure exerting the opposite effect on the determination of the optimum size of the plant to that which is logically required because at a given cost of capital higher costs over time result. The same applies to the cost of capital because a higher cost of capital would result in a smaller plant and again this aggravates the consequences of the lower profitability over time due to lower proceeds or higher cost.

In the build-up towards the optimum the PDV's of the cash flows of the various capacities may conceal situations in the intermediate steps which make an optimum different from that of the discounted cash flow, a logical proposition for further study as the basis for a decision.

The conclusion from this chapter is again that the one figure of PDV conceals far too much information in it for it to be used ex-

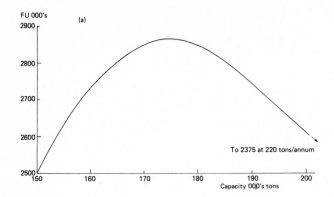

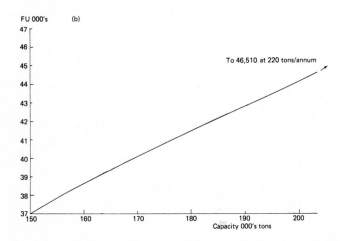

Graph 5.7. (a) The aggregates of the net income from year 1 to 7 of the various capacities of project 5.3. (b) The aggregates of the net capital employed from year 1 to 7 of the various capacities of project 5.3.

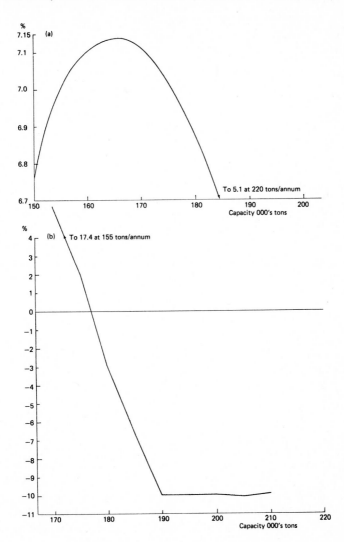

Graph 5.8. (a) The PIP of the various capacities of project 5.3. (b) The differential PIP's of stepwise increases in capacity of project 5.3.

TABLE 5.13

Optimum capacities suggested for project 5.3 using the major profitability criteria of pay-out time, discounted cash flow and financial accounts (in 000's tons).

POT	170	
EP/PDV	180	215
Financial		
accounts	165	175

clusively as a criterion for the selection of mutually exclusive projects. It also introduces an alien element in the analysis in that a discount rate is not directly relevant to building up sound financial accounts. The choice of the discount rate for which the solution may be very sensitive, is subjective in the same sense in which other basic data reflect subjective judgments. Thus an additional area in which subjective judgment has to be applied and which is irrelevant to the problem is introduced, thereby drawing attention away from the problem to which subjective judgment should be directly applied, e.g., the capacity of the plant. Discounted cash flow sidetracks the issue and is confusing.

Therefore in project evaluation there should be far more room for subjective judgment by those who have to take the decision, than the discounted cash flow allows. Indeed discounted cash flow carries by its very nature the image of making decisions easy and automatic, because if there is a choice of alternatives, the highest PDV will automatically win. Yet for all its convenience this may conceal very complicated situations which cannot be so easily summarised in one figure. Hidden under the surface there may be facts which are vital for the decision, e.g., the profitability in individual years. Blind and exclusive use of the discounted cash flow method would not allow these to be unearthed. Yet they are vital for the decision. The ultimate test ought to be the influence of the decision on the annual financial accounts and if the managers are informed on the alternatives in these terms, only then do they have the proper material for a sound decision. The role of judgment in project evaluation has been relegated into the background by the discounted cash flow. The financial accounts approach attempts to reinstate it to its proper place because they reproduce the figures in the accounts on which the company will ultimately be judged, and because they can highlight the factors for which the profitability is sensitive in individual years. Thus they can provide the correct basis for a decision on the most desirable alternative.

CHAPTER 6

DISCOUNTED CASH FLOW AND GROWTH

The problems of growth which any company has to face, can be found in the financial, technical, personnel, environmental and other fields. This study is confined entirely to the financial field, which of course reflects the other fields only to the extent that they can be quantified.

The problems which may arise have been very clearly described for the chemical industry by Sir Paul Chambers when he was Chairman of Imperial Chemical Industries:[9]

> '....At the end of 1965 we had about £ 200 million invested in plants which were either uncompleted or which were not yet in full operation, and therefore making little or no contribution to sales, and no contribution whatever to profits; indeed they were adding to costs. With about one fifth of our total capital invested in this way, the adverse effect on the rate of return on total capital has been substantial.

> It has taken longer than we expected to bring into full and efficient operation some new plants which were completed during the year. They are very large plants, incorporating new or modified processes and our experience that such plants take longer to bring into effective operation than expected, has been shared by chemical companies throughout the world....'

After discussing delays in the delivery of equipment for these plants by specialised suppliers he continues:

[9] See 'Review of ICI's Prospects', *The Sunday Times*, 3rd April, 1966.

'These twin problems of delays in getting large plants with novel processes completed, and further delay in getting such plants into full operation when they are completed, are not new, and, although they are more important today because the amount of capital involved is so large, we must avoid exaggeration. These plants take at least two or three years to design, fabricate and erect, and the amount of capital which your company has tied up in uncompleted plants, or in plants not in effective operation has always been considerable and is exceptionally large today because of the scale upon which capital expenditure has been sanctioned in the past two years....'

Every enterprise has to face to a greater or lesser degree problems of this kind when it expands. The factors which are at play and which affect the accounts and profitability of the company may be sum-marised in a more generalised form as follows:[10]

(1) During the building period, capital is tied up in a partially com-pleted production unit. This capital yields no return at all until the project is completed, and production (and sales) begin.
(2) Pre-operational expenses are incurred for example because the end-product is not immediately up to specification and/or person-nel must be trained to operate the equipment.
(3) The new production unit does not immediately operate at full capacity because the capacity of the unit has to allow for market growth. The result is that in the initial phases the overheads of the new production unit have to be spread over a smaller output which means higher unit costs.
(4) The book value of the invested capital is high in the initial years because during that period it benefits from only a few years of depreciation. As a result the new investment does not contribute as attractive a profitability in terms of NI/NCE to the overall result in the early years as in the later years.
(5) If an existing enterprise is taken over or a merger takes place, the

[10] I owe points 1–4 to Mr. J. van Embden.

various functions (production, marketing, accounts, etc.) of the enterprise to be taken over, or to be merged, have to be integrated as far as necessary with those of the parent company. This involves costs.

(6) If the new investment is financed by loans then interest payments will be higher in the early years than in the later years, because cash is generated over the years to pay off the loans and interest payments are reduced accordingly.

Factors 1–4 can be found in project 'P' (see Table 1.1 and Table 1.2). In years 1 and 2 (the building period) the following capital sums are tied up in partially completed plant (see line 31) (in FU 1000's):

Year 1   2984.4,
Year 2   5968.8.

There are no proceeds against this, but only costs–pre-operational expenses (line 10):

Year 2   89.5.

Pre-operational expenses continue in year 3 when operations commence:

Year 3   134.3.

The plant does not reach full capacity until year 8, the sixth year of operation (line 1). Sales develop as is shown in Table 6.1. The book value shows a peak in year 3 and declines steadily to year 12 when it is zero (see Table 6.2).

The influence of all these factors is reflected in a steadily increasing net income and NI/NCE as the project develops in time (see Table 6.3). It may be concluded that the new project has an adverse effect on the profitability of the company as a whole in the initial years steadily improving in later years.

However cases may also occur in which the net income of the new investment is high in the initial years and then falls in the later years. This would of course reduce considerably the depressing effect of the new investment on the profitability of the company as a whole, and

TABLE 6.1
Sales of project 'P' (see Table 1.1) from year 3 to year 8 in which full capacity is reached (in 000's tons).

Year	Sales
3	156.0
4	162.2
5	168.7
6	175.5
7	182.5
8	185.0

TABLE 6.2
The book value of project 'P' (see Table 1.2) (in FU 000's).

Year	Book value
1	2984.4
2	5968.8
3	6714.9
7	3730.5
11	746.1
12	0

may even improve it. Nevertheless whatever the time profile of net income, the following factors will always have a depressing effect on profitability and NI/NCE:

(1) investments locked up in partially completed plant;
(2) pre-operational expenses;
(3) a high book value in the initial years – a factor which always applies to every new investment;
(4) the costs of merging with another business;
(5) interest payments to finance any loans.

The influence of the principles of growth on the financial accounts can be further analysed by studying a growth model (see Graph 6.1).
The company as a whole consists in any one year of a number of

TABLE 6.3

The net income and NI/NCE of project 'P' (see Table 1.2) from year 2 to year 6.

Year	Net income (FU 000's)	NI/NCE (%)
2	(44.7)	(0.1)
3	454.6	5.6
4	518.5	7.1
5	571.0	8.6
6	624.9	10.5

investments which have been made in the past and are each in a different stage of development. Their profitability varies over time, and their stage of development determines whether it makes a positive or negative contribution towards the profitability of the company as a whole. The horizontal axis measures time (in years) and the length of the horizontal bars illustrates the time span between the inception of the project and the end of its life time. The vertical column with dotted outline represents the financial results of the company as a whole at the end of year 11, i.e., it is the sum total of the financial results of the various projects in their divergent stages of development. In year 10 the investment started in year 1 (project 1) has been retired. This initial investment has been called 'building brick'[11] – it is the model for an investment which is typical for the development of the business. Further investments in subsequent years have the same profitability pattern as 'building brick' but the investment in any one year (and consequently its proceeds and costs) has a scale $1 + G$ as large as the investment in the previous year – whereby G is the financial growth rate.

Analysing the situation in year 11, the project started in that year (project 11) is in the building stage where it makes no contribution to proceeds and only adds to the burden of the net capital employed of the business as a whole. Similarly although project 10 may have been mechanically completed, it may incur pre-operational expenses, e.g., due to the fact that the new process is not yet working satisfactorily

---

[11] I owe this description of the basic project to Mr. P.M. Inman.

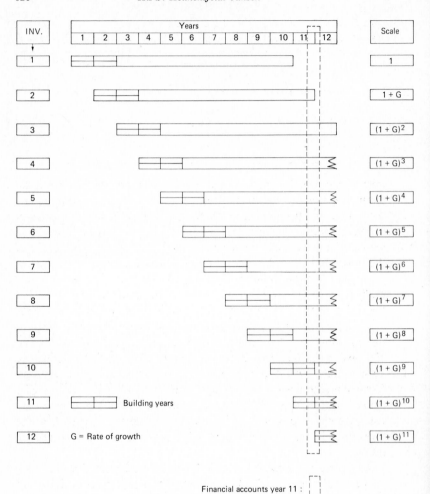

Graph 6.1. Growth and the financial accounts.

with a consequent waste of raw materials, steam electricity, etc. Again the processes used in projects 7 and 8 are probably running satisfactorily but their loading may not be up to full capacity because their capacity allows for growth of the market. In addition their book value would be relatively high, because they have only benefited from 3–4 years of depreciation. Projects 3 and 4 would probably be operating at full capacity and since they have been running for a considerable period, their book value would be low or zero.

Thus in year 11 investment 8–11 may have a depressing effect on the business because their financial results are lower than those of the business as a whole. This has to be more than compensated by the financial results of investments 2–7 if the overall result of the business is to show an acceptable level. The scale of investments 8–11 is greater than that of investments 2–7, and therefore their downpulling influence is correspondingly more severe. This is aggravated by the fact that even without scaling the net capital employed of investments 8–11 in their initial years is by its very nature higher than that of projects 2–7 in their later years, and this by itself constitutes a further downward force.

The time profile of the profitability contributed by individual projects may also be very different from what has been described. For instance the profitability may be high in the early years and low in the later years due to a high cash generation at first and a low cash generation later. Thus projects 7 to 9 would have a high profitability in year 11, and this would have to compensate for the lower profitability of investments 2 to 6. It may also have been necessary to invest during the course of the years in non-earning projects, e.g., for social amenities or anti-pollution measures. These would of course be a burden to the overall result and, apart from the reduction of their book value through time, they would show little variation in the (negative) profitability pattern which they contribute to the business.

The downward pulling effect of a new investment at a given NI/NCE is greater in any one year n, the greater is its scale in relation to the existing business. This is illustrated in Table 6.4.

It is supposed that the existing business has a net income of FU 120 and a net capital employed of FU 1000. Therefore the NI/NCE of the

TABLE 6.4

The size of the new investment in relation to the existing business and NI/NCE of the overall business (in FU's).

	Case A			Case B		
	NI	NCE	NI/NCE (%)	NI	NCE	NI/NCE (%)
Existing business	120	1000	12	120	1000	12
New investment	6	100	6	60	1000	6
Total	126	1100	11.4	180	2000	9.0

existing business in year n is 12%. In Case A the new investment has a net income in the same year n of FU 6, and a net capital employed of FU 100 and the resultant NI/NCE is 6%. The overall profitability of the business including the new investment is 11.4%.

In Case B the NI/NCE of the new investment in year n is again 6% but its scale is 10 times as large as in Case A. The resultant NI/NCE for the business as a whole including the new investment is 9%, as much as 2.4% lower than that of Case A. It follows again that the new investment should be studied against the background of the existing business. Discounted cash flow does not do this. It considers the new investment in isolation as 'an' investment. Furthermore it is not able to analyse the situation in a single year, as would be necessary in order to study the situation of year n as in this case.

From the analysis it also follows that financial results generated by a new investment in the early years should not be given more or less weight than financial results generated by the same investment in the later years, as the criteria of the discounted cash flow with their time preference do; for earning power over-emphasises the early years and under-emphasises the later years, and PDV may do the opposite. A given earning power may be achieved with very different levels of profitability (in accounting terms) in the early and later periods, and this has correspondingly very divergent results on the overall financial results of the company – again in accounting terms.[12] (These results

[12] See also Chapter 8.

also depend on the rate of growth.) Therefore equal weight should be given to the financial results of the new investment in both the earlier and later periods. Of course it is true that everything else being equal, early financial returns in the near future are to be preferred to late returns in the more distant and therefore more nebulous future. However, if the growth of the company were to be brought about by new investments which all show a feeble profitability in the later period, then that company tends to lose its ability to grow without its overall financial results falling to an unacceptable level, because it would not be able to carry the depressing effect of further investments, or to absorb any miscalculations. This means that in spite of the difficulties of making estimates for the more distant future it is essential to study the result of the later years just as much as those of the earlier years. Discounted cash flow glosses over this because by its very nature it only makes sense if all figures over the whole period are summarised into one figure, thus hiding the characteristic structure of that cash flow through time.

The cash position for the company as a whole is thus a resultant of the growth rate, and the cash contributions which each individual investment in its own stage of development makes to the overall position in any particular year. Thus the cash flow of any one project in any one year is blurred because the cash flow generated by one project is increased or reduced by the positive or negative cash flow generated by other projects in the same year and as a result that cash flow looses its identity. The principles are illustrated in Tables 6.5 and 6.6. If the cash flow shown in part A of Table 6.5 is taken as building brick, then the growth model for the company as a whole would show an overall cash position in year 4 at an assumed growth rate of 10% as shown in part B of the same table. Table 6.6 compares this cash position with that after a growth rate of 15%.

In spite of the fact that all investments have an earning power of 20%, the size of the cash flow generated by the company as a whole depends on the rate of growth but also on the interplay of the cash flows generated by the various investments in any one year. It follows that from the point of view of the well being of the company attention should be focussed in project evaluation not only on the cash flow of

TABLE 6.5

The cash flow of building brick and the overall cash position of company A before finance on the assumption that it grows at 10% per annum (in FU's).

(A) The cash flow of 'building brick'	
Year	Cash flow
1	(300)
2	170
3	140
4	105
EP (%)	20

(B) The cash flow of the company as a whole (before finance) assuming a 10% growth rate

Project 1	$105 \times 1 = 105$
2	$140 \times 1.1 = 154$
3	$170 \times 1.1^2 = 206$
4	$(300) \times 1.1^3 = (399)$
Cash position company as a whole:	66

individual projects through time as the criteria of the discounted cash flow do, but on the cash position of the company in any one year. Whilst the contribution of each particular investment to the overall position is important, the company faces the realities of its financial situation in relation to the outside world on the level of the business as a whole. Again the technique of the discounted cash flow glosses over this because it assesses the cash flow of the *individual* investment, the investment 'tel quel' without relating it to that of the business in corresponding years. Nor can in that light a criterion for the cash flow of an individual investment being satisfactory or unsatisfactory be laid down, because such a criterion only derives its meaning from the sum total of positive cash generated by other projects in the same year, and expenditure on new investments in that year. Cash may be surplus, in the company, or it may have to be invested in the money market to

TABLE 6.6
The cash generation of company A (before finance) on the assumption of a 10% and 15% growth rate.

Rate of growth: 10%

(300)	170	140	105			
	(330)	187	154	116		
		(363)	206	169	127	
			(399)	226	186	140

Cash surplus in year 4: 66

Rate of growth: 15%

(300)	170	140	105			
	(345)	196	161	121		
		(397)	225	185	139	
			(457)	259	213	160

Cash surplus in year 4: 34

generate interest, or it may be used to pay dividends, or it may be invested in new projects. It is in any event a means to running the business. Cash generated by the new project in a given year, is by itself no indication of its present or future role in the business. The desirable level is derived from the objectives of the company, and the study of growth normally plays an important part in the formulation of these objectives. However important cash is to the company, it is less through cash than through net income that the company projects its image to the financial world. To the extent that it is through cash that the company projects its image to the financial world, it is through the ability of cash to sustain growth, to create the means to generate an acceptable level of profitability, to pay dividends, etc., and by it to provide the means for its continued existence.

When the discounted cash flow is applied, the term 'cost of capital' is often loosely used in connection with the profitability of an individual project, and then it is tacitly made to apply to the company as a whole. However the company faces the problems of the cost of capital not on the level of the individual investment but on the level of the corporate entity. In the realities of the financial world the facets of the cost of capital which arise comprise not only the rate of interest on loans, to which the discounted cash flow almost entirely confines its attention, but also the size of the deficit which has to be financed, the length of the loan, and the redemption pattern. These facets apply on a corporate level. The theory of the discounted cash flow ignores that problem; its implications about the cost of capital apply to the individual project only and not to the corporate entity to which logically they should apply.

The cost of capital which the company can stand is therefore determined by the structure of the cash flow of individual projects, their profitability and the rate of growth. The influence of earning power and the rate of growth are illustrated in Table 6.7. The rate of interest on loans which the company can carry whilst breaking even – making no profit or loss – has been calculated for simple growth models with alternative earning powers for building brick and subsequent investments of 8%, 10% and 12% and for growth rates varying from 7 to 15%. It can be seen that the limit to the cost of capital which the company can carry is lower the faster is the rate of growth. For instance at an earning power of 10%, the break even rate of interest at a growth rate of 8% is higher than that at a growth rate of 15%. This is of course explained by the fact that more of the cash generated by investments in later stages of development is required to finance the new investments, and thus less is available to pay interest on loans. As would be expected the break even rate of interest at a given growth rate is higher, the higher is the earning power of building brick and subsequent investments. Even if all new investments have the same earning power as the original project 'building brick', and if they also have the same life times, then the interest on the loans which that company can carry without making a profit or loss, is always different from the earning power of the original project, and is only by coincidence equal to it.

However two situations can be visualised in which the cost of

TABLE 6.7

The interest on loans which the business as a whole could pay without making a profit or loss, if it is assumed that building brick and subsequent investments, has an 8%, 10% or 12% earning power and a growth rate as indicated (in %).[a]

Rate of growth (%)	After 45% tax			No tax		
	EP building brick, etc.					
	8%	10%	12%	8%	10%	12%
7	12.6	16.6	20.5	6.9	9.1	11.3
8	12.3	16.2	20.1	6.7	8.9	11.0
10	11.8	15.5	19.3	6.5	8.6	10.6
12	11.3	14.9	18.6	6.2	8.2	10.2
15	10.6	14.0	17.6	5.8	7.7	9.6

[a]It has been assumed that the life time of building brick and subsequent investment is 10 years; the rate of growth applies to fixed assets.

capital as handled by the discounted cash flow for an individual project, can in fact be applied to the entire company so that the earning power of the new investment sets an upper limit to the cost of capital which the company as a whole can carry. This occurs in the first place if the new project is added to an existing complex of which during the life time of the new project the aggregate cash flow each year is equal to zero. Clearly if this applies the earning power of the new project sets an upper limit to the rate of interest which the company can carry. A similar situation arises if the cash flow applies to a new and separate corporate entity whilst it is foreseen that during its life time no further cash flows generated by new projects will be associated with it. Under those conditions the cash flow would clearly stand by itself and apply to the corporate level. Either situation is of course most unlikely to occur in reality.

Summarising within the context of growth two different periods should be distinguished in the profitability pattern of individual investments, that in which the new investment is a burden to the overall result, and that in which its favourable results have to be able to carry the burdens of further new investments. The earning power principle with its properties of time preference over-emphasises the first period and under-emphasises the second, and the PDV principle may do the opposite, notwithstanding the fact that both periods are worth studying. Furthermore, in so far as cash flow problems and the cost of capital are concerned, the discounted cash flow limits its attention to the individual project although the company has to face the realities of the financial world on a corporate level. Discounted cash flow looks at the new investment in isolation. In fact the profitability performance of the individual project in terms of earning power with its attendant concept of the cost of capital, is entirely shrouded within the context of growth of the company as a whole because the maximum cost of capital, which the company can sustain depends apart from the earning power of individual projects on the rate of growth. This is a vital parameter which also deserves close attention. It plays an important role in the final outcome of the interplay between the cash flow – positive or negative – generated by new projects, and the cash flow generated in corresponding years by existing projects, and thus in the overall financial position of the company. Cash generated by the individual investment only derives its meaning from its interdependence with the cash generated by the company as a whole. Cash is of course vitally important (e.g., dividends) but more so as a means of running the business than as an end in itself. Its significance emanates from its ability to ensure the continued existence of the business, and its ability to assist in generating net income. The generation of net income must be the ultimate aim, and the rate of growth plays an important role in the achievement of that aim.

CHAPTER 7

AN ALTERNATIVE SUGGESTION – THE PIP, PAP AND PEP

The impact of the new investment on the profitability of the company is determined by its profitability characteristics (which have been analysed in Chapter 6) as well as by its size in relation to that of the existing business and the profitability of the existing business itself. All factors which are at play vary from case to case and they exert their influence on the overall profitability of the company after the new investment has been made, according to their size and nature.

Thus the forces at work create in each case their own situation with its own individual characteristics. It is therefore desirable to quantify the problem, and to calculate the net income, net capital employed and net income as a percentage of the net capital employed for both the new investment and the existing business, and then to add them together. The new investment is so to speak 'grafted' on to the existing business. This results in a detailed picture of the future financial situation on the assumption that the new investment is implemented. A comparison can then be made with the future financial situation on the assumption that the new investment is not implemented, and thus a firm basis for a profitability assessment of the new investment is obtained. The principle of the evaluation is: the company accounts with and without the new investment.

Although it is important for companies to do this from time to time according to the needs of the situation for all proposed investments, the method is clearly cumbersome for routine usage such as screening evaluations, even in the age of computers. A simpler method has to be evolved.

A first step towards a solution would be to calculate the net income (and loss) generated by the new investment along principles which are the same as those of the existing business. Clearly any losses would reduce by that amount overall net income, whilst conversely any net income would correspondingly increase it. Furthermore an analysis of net income (and losses) as a percentage of the net capital employed of the new investment over a number of years would show how long the profitability of the new investment would be a drag on the business because during the first years they might cause the overall results to be below the level they have been in the past, or below the level which is considered by the management to be the absolute minimum for the company to sustain its financial standing in the market. Conversely they may show to what extent the new investment may raise that percentage for the business as a whole above the minimum required so that further growth can be justified.

However a presentation of figures for net income and percentages for NI/NCE for separate years over a period which may well be 10 years or longer, is again a very cumbersome procedure. It may suit the specialist but it is certainly unsuitable for board submissions. A shorthand can however be introduced. It expresses the profitability of the individual project in terms of the financial results as shown in the accounts of the company. It fits in with the problems of growth outlined in the previous chapter, but it must be emphasised that it does not provide a complete solution.

The criterion distinguishes two periods in the existence of the new investment:

(1) The period during which its profitability has a depressing effect on the overall result – the *initial* period.
(2) The period during which its profitability is sufficiently high for it to be able to carry, in conjunction with the existing business, the depressing effect of later expansions, consistent with the overall result of the business remaining at an acceptable level. The profitability during this period – the period *after* the initial period – expresses the carrying capacity of the project, its ability to assist in carrying the depressive effect of further investments. This could be

called the 'biceps' of the new investment.

The two periods clearly play an entirely different role in the growth process of the company.

The situation as described can also be reversed in time so that the initial period constitutes the 'biceps' of the new project, and the later period constitutes a burden. In such cases every new investment is a stimulant to increasing profitability. However if a new investment is made, there are always certain factors which have a depressing effect in the initial years.

Three simple criteria can express the profitability performance of the new investment in the initial period, in the later period and in the entire period:

(1)   PIP = Profitability in the Initial Period.
(2)   PAP = Profitability After the Initial Period.
(3)   PEP = Profitability in the Entire Period of 1 and 2 together.

The PIP is defined as the weighted average of the net income as a percentage of the net capital employed during the period which commences when the first capital is spent on the project and terminates p years after the project has gone into operation; p can be taken as any number of years according to circumstances. The calculation of the PIP has been illustrated in Table 7.1 (p has been taken at 5 years).

The PAP is defined as the weighted average of the net income as a percentage of the net capital employed during the period which commences in year $p + 1$ and terminates q years thereafter; q can be taken as any number of years according to circumstances. In the example of Table 7.1 it has been taken as 5 years.

The PEP is defined as the weighted average of the net income as a percentage of the net capital employed during the period which commences when the first capital is spent on the project and terminates n years thereafter. This profitability indicator is parallel to the conventional earning power or PDV criterion in that it is expressed over the building years plus the operating life of the project (see Table 7.1).

The PIP, PAP and PEP have no accounting significance. They

TABLE 7.1
The calculation of the PIP, PAP and PEP (in FU's).

Year	NI	NCE	NI (cum.)	NCE (cum.)	NI (cum.)	NCE (cum.)	NI (cum.)	NCE (cum.)
1		1,500		1,500				1,500
2		3,250		4,750				4,750
3	(440)	4,200	(440)	8,950			(440)	8,950
4	240	3,790	(200)	12,740			(200)	12,740
5	375	3,379	175	16,119			175	16,119
6	436	3,153	611	19,272			611	19,272
7	541	2,900	1,152	22,172			1,152	22,172
8	541	2,550	PIP: 5.2%		541	2,550	1,693	24,722
9	541	2,200			1,082	4,750	2,234	26,922
10	541	1,850			1,623	6,600	2,775	28,772
11	541	1,500			2,164	8,100	3,316	30,272
12	541	1,150			2,705	9,250	3,857	31,422
					PAP: 29.2%		PEP: 12.3%	

have only been designed to give a summary – based on data as shown in the accounts – of the profitability during the three respective periods and they circumvent the need to express the profitability in a long series for individual years.

The PIP and PAP are in no way related to the cost of capital as discount percentages are purported to be. The criteria are really an indication of the shape and material of a building brick which the company can use and 'afford' in its growth pattern in which all the time it has to see to it that it 'constructs' healthy financial accounts. The desirable levels and relative size of the PIP and PAP may vary widely between individual firms and individual industries because they may reflect wide divergencies of economic structures between these companies and industries. For example, an investment project in a rubber plantation has to take account of the fact that it takes 5 years before the trees produce saleable latex. During that period interest to service the invested capital – if any – and the cost of maintaining the plantation is not compensated by the sales proceeds of the latex. When saleable latex becomes available, the production of the young trees is likely to be high and it falls after the first three years. Over the years the profitability of the plantation (i.e., the net income as a % of net capital employed) is likely to rise much slower than in manufacturing industry, because investment in land is not depreciated and it constitutes a major proportion of the total investment. In the light of these factors it would probably be logical to take in this case the length of the PIP period to include in addition to the period in which trees develop until they produce saleable latex, a 'productive' period of only 3 years thereafter. As a result the desirable PIP can only be low, because the maximum that can be achieved would be low. In comparison the profitability in the later period would be relatively much higher, because there are proceeds against the investment in every year.

This profitability structure can be compared with that of a new branch of a chain store, or new storage capacity for a basic commodity. In the latter case the building time would probably not exceed 18 months. It is likely that in such projects working capital such as stocks constitute a large proportion of the total investment, and since working capital is not depreciated, net income as a percentage of net capital employed is not likely to rise as fast as – say – in the case of an investment in a chemical plant, in which the amount of capital to be depreciated is very high in comparison with the working capital.

The PIP and PAP reflect the structure of the individual investments, 'building bricks', with which the company as a whole grows. These bricks should form an integral part of the building as a whole and they cannot be considered in isolation. Here lies the basic difference between the PIP and PAP approach and that of the discounted cash flow, because the discounted cash flow evaluates the project in isolation as an investment 'tel quel' without any consideration being given to the profitability of the business to which that investment is added. Whereas discounted cash flow relates the financial results generated by that investment over a sequence of years to each other 'horizontally', and leaves the evaluation at that, the PIP and PAP have been designed to relate those results not only 'horizontally' over the years, but also 'vertically' to the business as a whole in the corresponding years, i.e., the concept is to evaluate in a two-dimensional sense.

Unlike earning power and present day value, the PIP and PAP are devices which assist in building up acceptable balance sheets for the business as a whole as and when it grows over the years.

From the foregoing it follows that a cut-off criterion for the PIP and PAP can only be given after a thorough study of the basic data of new investments of the relative company, and against the background of the financial results of the existing business. The fundamental principle should always be that the financial results of the new investment(s) and those of the existing business should be 'brought together' so that a full picture is obtained of the effect of the new investment(s) on the financial results as a whole. Within that framework a cut-off point for the PIP and PAP can only be applied if there is a rhythmical growth pattern in the enterprise that is to say if the investment steps in that business can be fitted into one or more categories, each with their own financial structure, and therefore each with their own desirable PIP and PAP levels. If in the investments of the company such a rhythmical pattern cannot be distinguished, then every proposed investment has to be looked at on its own merits, i.e., the results of individual years have to be studied against the background of those of the existing business in the corresponding years. Only with the aid of a very thorough knowledge of the business, is it possible to decide whether a growth model of the enterprise with its individual investment steps on a rhythmical basis can be constructed. An even more difficult step – the construction of a model – must then follow. With all the uncertainties that the construction of such a model would have, it would still be, with careful and competent handling, of invaluable assistance in studying planning problems of the company.

From the fact that there may be wide divergencies between industries of the profitability structure of the successive investment steps, it follows that neither a universally desirable level of the PIP and PAP which applies to all industries, nor a generally desirable relationship between them can be given. In that respect the PIP and PAP approach differs again radically from that of the discounted cash flow, because in the latter method a cut off point is often defined in terms of the 'cost of capital' which is related to the capital market and is therefore of general application to industry at large. Yet for a wide variety of companies which all face the same capital market and which in other respects face roughly the same fiscal and other financial problems, very divergent PIP's and PAP's for their investments may be satisfactory because they face very different structural problems in the economic activities which they pursue in the course of satisfying market demand. The PIP and PAP are not related to the capital market but to economic structure in all its diversity.[13] The problem of the cost of capital to the company does not arise through the shape and nature of its individual investment steps, but through the annual accounts which are presented for the business *as a whole*. It is through these annual accounts that the company presents a face to the outside world and the continuity of the company can only be ensured if these accounts are healthy. A profitability analysis in terms of the PIP and PAP would go far to explain why it is right for certain enterprises to grow slower than the market. On a macro economic level it would be interesting to investigate to what extent the structure of industry could be explained in those terms.

Unlike the criteria of the discounted cash flow, the PIP and PAP do not pretend to be self-contained profitability criteria for investment proposals. In spite of the fact that they derive their significance, and permissible level from the financial results of the existing business to which the new investment is added, and thus in contrast to the criteria of the discounted cash flow relate the new investment to the existing business, they still consider the project in isolation if a full calculation of the profitability of the company as a whole, with and without the new investment, is not made. This follows from the fact that a desirable level of the PIP and PAP can only be determined against the background of the existing business. Furthermore the PIP and PAP do not incorporate, or provide, any information on the consequences of the rate of growth for the profitability. The financial growth rate is a most important further dimension. By their very nature the PIP and PAP bypass the fact that the implementation of too many projects *at the same time* may mean too heavy a burden for the overall profi-

---

[13] Compare with Chapter 2 where the relationship between the discounted cash flow and economic structure is discussed.

H.P.J. Heukensfeldt Jansen

tability even if all new projects have individually attractive PIP's and PAP's. Thus the individual building bricks may be attractive but the wall for which they have been used may be unacceptable because it

TABLE 7.2
The profitability and investment list – the PAIL (in FU's).

Part 1. Capital expenditure, working capital							
Project	DOC[a]	Capital expenditure[b]	Years				
			1	2	3	4	5
'A'	1–7–1	18,000	1,800				
'B'	1–4–5	17,800		2,900	7,030	6,150	1,760
'C'	1–7–4	9,000			2,700	5,400	900
'D'	1–1–5	1,600			600	800	200
'E'	1–1–5	20,000		1,600	6,800	8,400	3,200
'F'	1–7–2	3,000	1,200	300			
'G'	1–4–4	10,000	800	3,400	4,200	1,600	
Capital expenditure			3,800	8,200	21,330	22,350	6,060
Add: working capital			4,456	910	536	4,740	6,975
Total			8,256	9,110	21,866	27,090	13,035

Part 2. Net income (losses)							
Project	PIP (%)	PAP (%)	PEP (%)	Years			
				1	2	3	4	5
'A'	3.1	21.7	8.9	(760)	(44)	702	1,466	2,197
'B'	6.1	33.4	11.7		(138)	(138)	(270)	56
'C'	3.5	30.8	12.1		(33)	(715)	(230)	395
'D'	11.7	21.8	15.4					213
'E'	5.8	21.5	11.2				(332)	(8)
'F'	neg.	neg.	neg.		(80)	(160)	(160)	(160)
'G'	4.1	17.0	8.6			(166)	(4)	270
NI (losses) investments				(760)	(295)	(477)	470	2,963
NI (losses) existing business				6,252	6,644	7,992	8,655	8,800
NI (losses) total				5,492	6,349	7,515	9,125	11,763
NI (losses) objectives				5,600	6,300	8,125	9,450	11,300

TABLE 7.2 (continued)

Part 3. Source and disposition of funds

	Years				
	1	2	3	4	5
Source of funds					
Net income	5,492	6,349	7,515	9,125	11,763
Depreciation	4,774	5,861	7,220	8,505	10,973
Total	10,266	12,210	14,735	17,630	22,736
Disposition of funds					
Capital expenditure	3,800	8,200	21,330	22,350	6,060
Working capital investments	4,456	910	536	4,740	6,975
Working capital existing business	520	120	50		
Total	8,776	9,230	21,916	27,090	13,035
Surplus (deficit)	1,490	2,980	(7,181)	(9,460)	9,701

[a]Date of completion.
[b]Total cost of the project.
neg. = negative.

has been built with too much haste. Therefore all investments should be put against the background of the existing business. There is nothing for it but to make periodically an overall profitability forecast of the company over a number of years including all new investments so as to ensure that the investment programme does not exceed acceptable limits.

A routine system for companies to keep track of the growth problems which have been described would probably vary widely from case to case, because the structure of industry is very heterogeneous, and with it the significance, size and complexity of the growth problems. However as an illustration a possible system which would probably only suit larger companies is shown in Table 7.2. Details are as follows: The system is called

Profitability And Investment List – PAIL

The list is subdivided into three parts:

Part 1. Capital expenditure.

Part 2. Net income and losses generated by the investment.

Part 3. The source and disposition of funds for the business as a whole including the new investments.

Part 1 lists the planned capital expenditure for individual projects which are either being built or for which plans exist. For example project 'A' of which the total cost is FU 18,000 is nearly completed and FU 1800 is still to be spent. Project 'D' is expected to cost FU 1600 of which FU 600 would be spent in year 3, FU 800 in year 4 and FU 200 in year 5. Totals to be spent each year including the working capital which is expected to be associated with the new projects are also given.

Part 2 lists the PIP, PAP and PEP of the planned investments. The net income and losses which are expected to be generated by them are also listed. These are added to those of the existing business and compared with the objectives.

Part 3 shows the source and disposition of funds for the company as a whole assuming that the new investments will be implemented. The resulting overall surpluses and deficits are of importance.

From Part 1 it can be seen that the company has committed itself to project 'A', and all but FU 1,800 has been spent. The plant is due to start operations in year 1, i.e., the year following the current one. The project has a very low PIP of only 3.1% (see Part 2) but it is expected that its net income will improve substantially in later years (see Table 7.3).

In common with project 'A', the other projects generate losses in the initial years. The net result is that the new investments together generate losses until the net income of project 'A' in years 4 and 5 is sufficiently high for the total of the net income of all new investments to be positive in those years (see Table 7.4).

Part 2 also shows that the net income of the company as a whole

TABLE 7.3
The net income of project 'A' (in FU's).

Year	Net income
1	(760)
2	(44)
3	702
4	1,466
5	2,197

TABLE 7.4
The total of the net income of all new investments (in FU's).

Year	Net income
1	(760)
2	(295)
3	(477)
4	470
5	2,963

after the new investments have been implemented, is lower than, or (in year 2) equal to that set for the objectives. Only in year 5 is it higher (see Table 7.5).

The source and disposition of funds (Part 3) shows surpluses in years 1, 2 and 5 and substantial deficits in years 3 and 4 (see Table 7.6).

In the judgment of the management this investment programme may well be too heavy a burden for the company.[14] The total net income of the new investments only becomes positive in the later years because one project (project 'A') generates substantial profits in those years. If for any reason the profitability of project 'A' does not come up to expectations, then the positive counterweight to the losses of the remaining projects is no longer available, and the overall result is vulnerable to it. This is the more important because the profitability level set by the objectives is higher in years 3 and 4 than that of the

[14]It is 'beyond the pale'.

H.P.J. Heukensfeldt Jansen

TABLE 7.5

A comparison of the estimated net income of the company (including new investments) and the objectives (in FU's).

Year	Net income	Objectives
1	5,492	5,600
2	6,349	6,300
3	7,515	8,125
4	9,125	9,450
5	11,763	11,300

TABLE 7.6

The source and disposition of funds of the company as a whole (including the new investments) (in FU's).

Year	Surplus (deficit) on source and disposition of funds
1	1,490
2	2,980
3	(7,181)
4	(9,460)
5	9,702

business as a whole, after all investments have been implemented. Furthermore it may well be that the company is not able to finance the large deficits in years 3 and 4 at least in so far as this can be anticipated in the present year.

If the investment programme has to be cut, then project 'C' would presumably be high on the list for removal or postponement, because it has a low PIP of 3.5%. Project 'F' can however not be removed in spite of the fact that it shows losses. The reason is that it consists of various investments to deal with environmental problems, i.e., water purification and anti air pollution, and the company has to carry them out in order to enable it to continue its business. The project will only cost money (= depreciation). Project 'E' could be removed or postponed for one year. So could project 'G'.

The net income position and the surplus position of the source and disposition of funds in year 5 allow for an increase in the downward pressure of new investments that year. Therefore postponement of projects to increase the burdens in year 5 would be justified.

The example illustrates that a PIP of 3.5% (project 'C') which may not be acceptable in this instance, may be acceptable in other circumstances, i.e., against a background of a higher net income of the existing business, or if there were some more projects like 'D' which do not generate a loss in the year of start up (e.g., investments for increasing existing capacity). It also illustrates that a universal cut-off point for the PIP and PAP cannot be defined, because the desirable level can only be determined within the context of the financial situation of the company as a whole in the corresponding years. Each given investment has to be studied separately within that context.

The author is well aware of the practical difficulties of putting together the PAIL. The frequency, the cost, the quality of the basic data which go into it, the precise information it should highlight and many other factors would have to be considered in the light of the problems with which the company in question is faced. The conclusion may well be that considerable simplification is required. Nevertheless a routine list of projects would highlight to the management the areas where judgment is needed and careful consideration is essential.

Summarising, the financial consequences of new investments should always be seen against the background of the accounts of the business as a whole, and the situation in individual years should be analysed. However, it would be very cumbersome to report the attractiveness of a new investment by giving separate figures for say 10 individual years. It has therefore been suggested that the profitability be summarised by giving the weighted average of the NI/NCE for two separate periods, i.e., (1) the profitability in the initial period – the PIP – and (2) the profitability after the initial period – the PAP.

Two separate periods have been distinguished because they play very different roles in the growth process; the period in which the new investment is likely to be a burden to the overall result, and the period in which the profitability has to be high enough for it to carry the burdens of further investment, without the overall result being reduced to unacceptable levels. The PIP and PAP have been designed to quantify the profitability of the new investment in those terms. They reflect the structure of the enterprise and the industry to which they apply in three parameters: the length of the PIP and PAP periods, their absolute levels, and their levels relative to each other. In other words, they describe the shape of the individual building brick with which the company grows – at least if a regular rhythm in the growth can be discerned. In all cases, whether there is a regular rhythm or not, it is imperative that the new investments and their financial consequences are periodically 'grafted' on to the existing business for the overall situation to be studied. In that light the limits for a cut off point become blurred because a lower limit can only be set against the latest available forecast background of the overall situation. A low PIP is only acceptable if the overall situation is favourable; conversely a high PIP is essential if the overall situation does not allow heavy burdens. Only a list of planned investments on a routine basis set against the background of the existing business and the objectives defined by the management, would ensure that the plans are kept under constant review to the benefit of the overall results. However the practical difficulties should not be ignored.

CHAPTER 8

EARNING POWER AND FINANCIAL GROWTH MODELS

The relationship between the basic 'building brick'[15] with which the company grows, and the overall profitability of the company, is determined by the growth rate, by the earning power of building brick, and by its PIP, PAP and PEP. It is essential to include the latter three parameters in the definitions of building brick, because a given earning power can be achieved with any combination between them, and their relative size at that earning power and at that growth rate determines the NI/NCE for the company as a whole. A description of building brick which is confined to earning power only, and which therefore implies a model with any relative values of the PIP, PAP and PEP is – though useful – of interest for special cases only in which the growth rate and cash surplus (or deficits) play their part. This chapter studies the nature of building brick in the growth process, its bearing on the construction of financial growth models, and the use of growth models for balance sheet analysis.

(The small differences in the percentages, sometimes as small as decimals of percentages to which importance has been attached in this chapter, may well be thought to be within the margin of error of the forecast. This is true. However the object of this chapter is to study the structural problems of growth in relation to the overall company result, and within that context the significance of the differences has again been ignored.)

In order to investigate what role the earning power of building brick, and subsequent investment steps, plays in the growth process,

[15]For a definition of building brick see Chapter 6.

models have been used which are identical in their basic design to that
of Graph 6.1. It may be recalled that the growth model was obtained
by adding each year to a basic investment with a given earning power
('building brick'), further models which have the same earning power
and a scale $1 + G$ as large as that of the previous year. When the life
time of building brick has been completed a dynamic equilibrium sets
in, and the financial details at that point represent the financial results
of the company as a whole.

The principles can be illustrated by a simple example.

The earning power of the following cash flow is 10% (in FU's)

$$
\begin{array}{ll}
\text{Year 1} & (1000) \\
\text{Year 2} & 555 \\
\text{Year 3} & 600
\end{array}
$$

It follows that

$$(1000) \times (1.1)^2 + 555 \times 1.1 + 600 \times 1 = 0.$$

The company cash flow in year 3 assuming a 10% growth rate is as
shown in Table 8.1. The terms of the addition to obtain the aggregate
cash flow are identical to those for the calculation of the earning
power of building brick because the total financial surplus or deficit is
equal to the aggregate of the cash flows generated by each project in
its own stage of development in that particular year after the necessary scaling by 1.1.

TABLE 8.1

The cash flow of company K in year 3 assuming a growth rate of 10% (in FU's).

Project	Scale	Years		
		1	2	3
1	1.0	(1000)	555	600
2	1.1		(1100)	610
3	$(1.1)^2$			(1210)
				0

A more general illustration is given in Table 8.2, Part A and Part B. The calculation of the financial surplus (or deficit) at a growth rate G, and the calculation of the earning power of building brick S are really identical operations with identical data, except for S and G. It follows that if $S = G$ the aggregate financial surplus (or deficit) in year n is equal to 0. The following rule applies:

If the earning power of building brick and subsequent investments is equal to the growth rate, then the company as a whole breaks even in its cash position on the source and disposition of funds. Therefore the company is self-financing at that growth rate.

The rule follows from the way the growth model has been constructed. It is really a tautology.

It may now be asked what influence the PIP, PAP and PEP of building brick and subsequent investments have at a given earning power, on the company NI/NCE, and what the company NI/NCE would be if the earning power of building brick is equal to the growth rate.

TABLE 8.2 (Part A)

The growth rate at which there is neither a surplus or deficit on the source and disposition of funds of the company.

	Years					
	1	2	...	$n-2$	$n-1$	n
Cash flow of building brick:	A	B	...	X	Y	Z
Discounted cash flow at S if EP $= S$:	$\dfrac{A}{1+S}$	$\dfrac{B}{(1+S)^2}$	...	$\dfrac{X}{(1+S)^{n-2}}$	$\dfrac{Y}{(1+S)^{n-1}}$	$\dfrac{Z}{(1+S)^n}$
						$\sum = 0$
Equation 1 (after multiplying by $(1 + S)^{n+1}$):	$A(1+S)^n$	$B(1+S)^{n-1}$	...	$X(1+S)^3$	$Y(1+S)^2$	$Z(1+S)$
						$\sum = 0$

TABLE 8.2 (Part B)

The relationship between the earning power of building brick (and subsequent investments) and the growth rate (G = growth rate in %).

1	2	...	$n-3$	$n-2$	$n-1$	n	Scale
		Years					
$A(1+G)$	$B(1+G)$	...	...	$X(1+G)$	$Y(1+G)$	$Z(1+G)$	$1+G$
	$A(1+G)^2$	$B(1+G)^2$	...	...	$X(1+G)^2$	$Y(1+G)^2$	$(1+G)^2$
		$A(1+G)^3$	$B(1+G)^3$	...	...	$X(1+G)^3$	$(1+G)^3$
			$A(1+G)^4$	...	...	...	$(1+G)^4$
				$B(2+G)^4$	...	...	$(1+G)^4$
				$A(1+G)^{n-1}$	...	$B(1+G)^{n-1}$	$(1+G)^{n-1}$
						$A(1+G)^n$	$(1+G)^n$

Sum total=0, if $S=G$
(see equation 1 of Part A)

Σ

A given earning power can be achieved by any combination of PIP's, PAP's and PEP's. This is illustrated by the models shown in Table 8.3. Each project has 2 pre-operational years and 10 operating years. At a given earning power there are sets of 5 projects which have successively a faster sales build-up to full capacity. These Cases have been called Case A, B, C, D and E. Thus in Case A the sales build up is very slow, and in Case E the plant is at full capacity from start up. For example the assumed sales build up for Cases A, C and E is as shown in Table 8.4.

It follows that for Case A the PIP is relatively low and the PAP relatively high, whilst for Case E the opposite is true. However all Cases A–E have the same earning power, and this has been achieved by adjusting the netback. For example for Cases A, C and E, the combination of PIP's, PAP's and PEP's, which are possible at an earning power of 9.5% are shown in Table 8.3 (Group 2) and Table 8.5.

Similar sets of data have been collected for three earning powers, i.e.,

	Earning power (%)
Group 1	7.5
2	9.5
3	11.5

TABLE 8.3

The influence of the PIP and PAP (at a given earning power of building brick) on the NI/NCE of the company as a whole at various growth rates (in FU's). Life time of the investment: 10 years.

Sales build up	A	B	C	D	E
% of capacity first two years towards full capacity	20–40 etc.	40–55 etc.	60–70 etc.	80–85 etc.	100–100 etc.

	Characteristics of investments in terms of profitability					Corresponding NI/NCE at various growth rates G (in %)					
	A	B	C	D	E	GR	A	B	C	D	E
Group 1											
						7.0	7.1	7.0	7.0	6.9	6.9
						7.5	6.9	6.9	6.9	6.9	6.9
EP %	7.5	7.5	7.5	7.5	7.5	8.0	6.8	6.8	6.8	6.8	6.9
PIP %	1.9	3.1	4.0	4.8	5.5	10.0	6.2	6.3	6.4	6.4	6.6
PAP %	25.4	21.7	18.5	15.7	13.2	12.0	5.6	5.9	6.2	6.3	6.4
PEP %	9.2	8.9	8.5	8.1	7.8	15.0	4.9	5.2	5.6	5.8	6.1
Group 2											
						7.0	9.6	9.4	9.2	9.1	9.0
						8.0	9.3	9.1	9.0	8.9	8.9
EP %	9.5	9.5	9.5	9.5	9.5	9.5	8.7	8.7	8.7	8.7	8.7
PIP %	3.5	4.8	5.7	6.5	7.1	10.0	8.5	8.5	8.5	8.6	8.6
PAP %	30.8	26.6	23.0	19.8	17.1	12.0	7.9	8.0	8.1	8.2	8.3
PEP %	12.1	11.6	11.1	10.5	10.1	15.0	7.0	7.3	7.5	7.7	7.9
Group 3											
						7.0	12.3	11.9	11.6	11.3	11.1
						8.0	11.8	11.5	11.3	11.1	10.9
EP %	11.5	11.5	11.5	11.5	11.5	10.0	11.0	10.9	10.8	10.7	10.6
PIP %	5.3	6.5	7.5	8.2	8.8	11.5	10.3	10.3	10.3	10.3	10.3
PAP %	36.3	31.6	27.5	23.9	20.9	12.0	10.2	10.3	10.3	10.3	10.3
PEP %	15.2	14.5	13.7	13.0	12.5	15.0	9.2	9.4	9.6	9.7	9.8

TABLE 8.4

An illustration of the sales build-up of Cases A, C and E shown in Table 8.3 (in tons).

Year	Cases		
	A	C	E
1	20	60	100
2	40	70	100
3	60	80	100
4	80	90	100
5	100	100	100

Table 8.5

The combination of PIP's, PAP's and PEP's which are possible at an earning power of 9.5% for Cases A, C and E of Table 8.3 (in %).

	Cases		
	A	C	E
EP	9.5	9.5	9.5
PIP	3.5	5.7	7.1
PAP	30.8	23.0	17.1
PEP	12.1	11.1	10.1

In each group there are 5 different cases, and thus 15 different models for cash flow calculations have been made. Each of them has been used as a building brick for the growth of the company.

Using these models as a basis for further study, it should in the first place be noted that the aggregate NI/NCE falls as the rate of growth increases (see also Graph 8.1). To take an example, for models with the sales build up of Case C, and an earning power of 11.5% the aggregate NI/NCE at increasing growth rates is as follows:

Growth rate (%)	Aggregate NI/NCE (%)
7	11.6
10	10.8
12	10.3
15	9.6

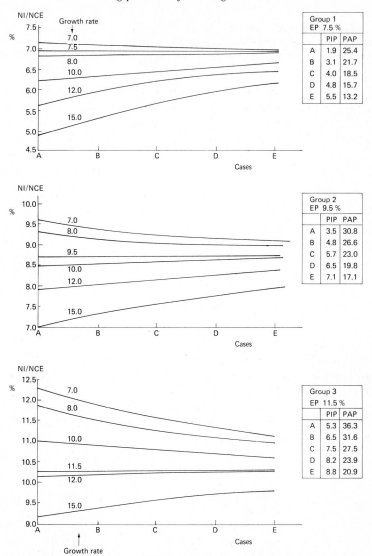

Graph 8.1. The influence of the PIP and PAP at various growth rates (and a given EP of building brick and subsequent investments) on the NI/NCE of the company.

The reasons for this have been analysed in Chapter 6.

The aggregate NI/NCE is (at a given earning power) more sensitive to the growth rate at a low PIP (and a high PAP) than at a high PIP and a low PAP. In other words if the PIP is low, its downpulling effect in the growth process is relatively greater in relation to the upholding effect of the correspondingly higher PAP. The 'biceps' of building brick is so to speak weaker than if the PIP were higher and the corresponding PAP lower. The following table illustrates this (in percentages):

Case	A	E
Earning power	7.5	7.5
PIP	1.9	5.5
PAP	25.4	13.2
Aggregate NI/NCE		
at a growth rate of 7%	7.1	6.9
at a growth rate of 15%	4.9	6.1
Reduction aggregate		
NI/NCE	2.2	0.8

In Case A the NI/NCE is reduced from 7.1% to 4.9%, i.e., by 2.2% as a result of an increase of the growth rate from 7% to 15%. The comparable figure for Case E in which the PIP is higher and the PAP is lower, is a reduction of the NI/NCE by 0.8%.

Furthermore the sensitivity of the NI/NCE to the growth rate is higher at a high earning power than at a low earning power of building brick and subsequent investments (in percentages)

Case	C	C
Earning power	7.5	11.5
Aggregate NI/NCE		
at a growth rate of 7%	7.0	11.6
at a growth rate of 15%	5.6	9.6
Reduction aggregate		
NI/NCE	1.4	2.0

If Case C has an earning power of 7.5%, the NI/NCE is reduced by 1.4% as a result of the increase in the growth rate from 7% to 15%. If however Case C has an earning power of 11.5% the reduction of the NI/NCE as a consequence of the same increase in the growth rate is 2.0%.

At a given earning power of building brick and subsequent investments, and at low growth rates, a low PIP and a high PAP produce a higher aggregate NI/NCE than a high PIP and a low PAP (see Table 8.3 and Graph 8.1). In other words at low growth rates the downpulling effect of a low PIP is relatively smaller in relation to the upholding effect of the correspondingly higher PAP. The 'biceps' of building brick is so to speak stronger than if the PIP were higher and the corresponding PAP lower. Thus at low growth rates the higher PAP overcomes the stronger downward pulling effect of the lower PIP. Panel I of the following table illustrates this (in percentages):

	Case	A	E
(I)	Earning power	11.5	11.5
	Growth rate	7.0	7.0
	PIP	5.3	8.8
	PAP	36.3	20.9
	Aggregate NI/NCE	12.3	11.1
(II)	Earning power	11.5	11.5
	Growth rate	15	15
	PIP	5.3	8.8
	PAP	36.3	20.9
	Aggregate NI/NCE	9.2	9.8

At a growth rate of 7% the NI/NCE of Case A at 12.3% is higher than that of Case E at 11.1% in spite of the fact that Case A has the lower PIP.

At the higher growth rate of 15% the reverse is true and a higher NI/NCE results with a high PIP and a correspondingly lower PAP, than a low PIP and a correspondingly higher PAP (in percentages), as shown in panel II of the above table.

At a growth rate of 15% Case A with a PIP of 5.3% has a NI/NCE of 9.2%, whilst Case E with the higher PIP of 8.8% has a NI/NCE of 9.8%.

If at slow growth rates the downward pull of a low PIP is overcome by a correspondingly high PAP, and at high growth rates the reverse is true, then there must be a growth rate at which the company NI/NCE is independent of the PIP and PAP and therefore equal for all cases A–E. The growth rate at which this occurs has been called the 'critical growth rate', and it turns out that it is equal to the earning power of building brick (see also Graph 8.1). The following table illustrates the earning power (EP), critical growth rate (CGR), and the aggregate NI/NCE which results for all Cases A–E (in percentages):

	EP	CGR	Aggregate NI/NCE
Group 1	7.5	7.5	7.0
Group 2	9.5	9.5	8.7
Group 3	11.5	11.5	10.3

The aggregate NI/NCE can be expressed in terms of the earning power of building brick (S) or the growth rate (G) to which it is equal. It is calculated for all Cases A to E for groups 1–3 as follows:[16]

$$\text{Group 1} \quad \frac{0.075}{1 + 0.075} = \frac{S}{1 + S} = \frac{G}{1 + G} = 0.07,$$

$$\text{Group 2} \quad \frac{0.095}{1 + 0.095} = \frac{S}{1 + S} = \frac{G}{1 + G} = 0.087,$$

$$\text{Group 3} \quad \frac{0.115}{1 + 0.115} = \frac{S}{1 + S} = \frac{G}{1 + G} = 0.103.$$

[16]It is known to me that this relationship was found independently by Mr. S.J.Q. Robinson.

The formula only applies if there are no dividend or interest payments because these payments are also left out of account in an ordinary cash flow calculation. A general proof of the rule is given in Appendix 1. It can also be illustrated by the use of a simple example (in FU's).

The following cash flow has an earning power of 10%:

    Year 1   (1000)
    Year 2   555
    Year 3   600

Therefore:

$$1000 = \frac{555}{1.1} + \frac{600}{(1.1)^2} \, ,$$

or:

$$600 + (555 \times 1.1) = 1000 \times (1.1)^2. \tag{1}$$

The investment of FU 1000 of building brick represents expenditure on a plant, which is written off in two years. The details of building brick are as follows (in FU's):

	1	2	3
Cash flow	(1000)	555	600
Cash generation		555	600
Depreciation		500	500
Net income		55	100

The net income of project 1 in year 3 is:

    FU 600 − FU 500 = FU 100.

The net income of project 2 in year 3 is 10% larger:

$$FU \ (555 - 500) \ (1.1).$$

Thus the aggregate net income in year 3 is:

$$FU \ 600 - 500 + (555 \times 1.1) - (500 \times 1.1).$$

It is known from the earning power equation (see equation 1) that:

$$FU \ 1000 \times (1.1)^2 = FU \ 600 + 555 \times 1.1.$$

Therefore the aggregate net income in year 3 is equal to:

$$FU \ 1000 \times (1.1)^2 - 500 - (500 \times 1.1).$$

However the depreciation of FU 500 is equal to:

$$FU \ \frac{1000}{2}$$

because the capital expenditure is FU 1000, and the depreciation period is 2 years.

Therefore the aggregate net income in year 3 is:

$$FU \ 1000 \times (1.1)^2 - \frac{1000}{2} \ (1.1) - \frac{1000}{2}$$

After dividing by 1000 and multiplying by 2 this becomes:

$$FU \ 2 \times (1.1)^2 - 1.1 - 1.$$

The corresponding net capital employed of building brick consists of:

Year 1:   the completed plant before it has gone into operation;
Year 2:   the book value of the plant, i.e., FU 1000 – FU 500;
Year 3:   the book value of the plant which is then zero.

Therefore the net capital employed in years 1, 2 and 3 is as follows (in FU's):

	1	2	3
Net capital employed building brick:	1000	500	0

The aggregate net capital employed in year 3 is as follows (in FU's):

Project 1:   0,

Project 2: $(1.1) \times 1000 - \dfrac{1000}{2} \times 1.1,$

Project 3: $(1.1)^2 \times 1000;$

Aggregate
NCE: $(1000)\,(1.1)^2 + (1000)\,(1.1) - \left(\dfrac{1000}{2}\right) \times (1.1).$

If this is divided by 1000 and multiplied by 2 the equation is:

$$2\,(1.1)^2 + 2 \times 1.1 - 1.1.$$

The aggregate NI/NCE is the ratio between (2) and (3):

$$\frac{2 \times (1.1)^2 - 1.1 - 1}{2\,(1.1)^2 + 2 \times 1.1 - 1.1} = \frac{2 \times (1.1)^2 - 2.2 + 0.1}{1.1\,(2 \times 1.1 + 1)}$$

$$= \frac{2.2\,(1.1 - 1) + 0.1}{1.1\,(2 \times 1.1 + 1)} = \frac{0.1}{1.1}$$

$$= \frac{S}{1 + S} = \frac{G}{1 + G}.$$

This ratio also applies separately to the following ratio in year n:
The cost of plant completed in year n, minus the aggregate depreciation in year n, divided by the aggregate book value in year n.
In the example, new plant to a total value of:

$$FU\ 1000 \times 1.1^2 = 1210,$$

has gone into operation in year 3.
The aggregate depreciation in that year is (in FU's):

Project 1:		500
Project 2:	$500 \times 1.1 =$	550
Aggregate depreciation:		1050

Project 1:		0
Project 2:	$500 \times 1.1 =$	550
Project 3:	$1000 \times (1.1)^2 =$	1210
Aggregate book value:		1760

Thus the cost of plant completed in year 3 minus the company depreciation in year 3 divided by the company book value in year 3 is

$$\frac{1210 - 1050}{1760} = \frac{160}{1760} = 0.909 = \frac{S}{1 + S} = \frac{G}{1 + G}.$$

In the cash flow which has been studied so far, it has been assumed that the investment is in respect of equipment which is depreciated. It can also be assumed that the investment consists entirely of working capital which of course is not depreciated. In the following cash flow for building brick which has an earning power of 10% (in FU's):

	1	2	3	4
Project 1:	(400)	(600)	235	1000

it has been assumed that an amount of FU 400 is invested in working capital in year 1, and a further amount of FU 600 in year 2. The built up working capital of FU 1000 is realised in year 4. The net income of building brick is (in FU's):

	1	2	3	4
Project 1:	0	0	235	0

Therefore the aggregate net income in year 4 is:

FU $1.1 \times 235 = 258.$

The aggregate net capital employed in that year is (in FU's):

Project 1:		0
Project 2:	1000×1.1	$= 1100$
Project 3:	1000×1.1^2	$= 1210$
Project 4:	400×1.1^3	$= 532$

Aggregate NCE: 2842

Therefore the aggregate NI/NCE is:

$$\frac{258}{2842} = \frac{0.1}{1.1} = \frac{G}{1+G} = \frac{S}{1+S}.$$

Thus the ratio also applies if the investment consists entirely of working capital. Equally it applies if the investment consists partly of machinery and equipment, and partly of working capital.

If:

W = the built-up working capital of building brick = 1000.

n = life time of building brick = 4,

m = number of years during which working capital is built up to the full amount = 2,

G = the growth rate = 10%,

then:

$$\frac{W(1 + G)^{n-m} - W}{W(1 + G)^{n-m} + \quad ... \quad + W(1 + G)} = \frac{G}{1 + G}$$

$$= \frac{S}{1 + S} \; .$$

The denominator shows the aggregate working capital excluding any portions (scaled to the appropriate level) which go towards the build up of W; thus in the example excluding:

FU 400 × (1.1) n.

Filling in the data of the example into the above equation:

$$\frac{1000 \times 1.1^2 - 1000}{1000 \times (1.1)^2 + 1000 \times 1.1} = \frac{210}{2310} = \frac{0.1}{1.1}$$

$$= \frac{G}{1 + G} = \frac{S}{1 + S}$$

Similar ratios apply to other constituents of the cash flow computation (or source and disposition of funds) of building brick, e.g., the separate amounts of capital expenditure each year which go into the build up to the full cost of the plant if the expenditure on the plant is spread over more than one year; or the separate amounts of working capital each year which go into the build up of the total working capital, if the build up to the full amount is spread over more than one year. The analysis of appendix 1 illustrates the details.

Summarising this chapter the following rules can be formulated:

If the growth process of the company is described by investments each year which generate the same earning power S, and which have a scale $1 + G$ as large as that in the previous year (whereby G is the rate of growth), and if $S = G$, then the following applies in year n when the dynamic equilibrium has set in:

Rule 1: There is no financial surplus or deficit on the company source and disposition of funds, and the company breaks even.

Rule 2: The company NI/NCE is equal to:

$$\frac{G}{1 + G} = \frac{S}{1 + S}.$$

Rule 3: The company NI/NCE is independent of the PIP and PAP.

Rule 4: The company NI/NCE is independent of the depreciation period.

Rule 5: The cost of plant completed in year n (C_n) minus the company depreciation in year n (Dep.), both divided by the company book value in year n (B), therefore:

$$\frac{C_n - \text{Dep.}}{B}$$

is equal to:

$$\frac{G}{1 + G} = \frac{S}{1 + S}.$$

Rule 6: The built-up working capital of building brick (W) on a scale equal to the number of years (k) in the life time of building brick in which it carried the full working capital W, therefore:

$$W(1 + G)^k$$

minus the built-up working capital on a scale $= 1$, therefore:

$$W$$

both factors divided by the aggregate in year n of built-up working capital, therefore:

$$W(1 + G)^k + \quad ... \quad + W(1 + G)$$

thus in total:

$$\frac{W(1 + G)^k - W}{W(1 + G)^k + \quad ... \quad + W(1 + G)}$$

is equal to:

$$\frac{G}{1 + G} = \frac{S}{1 + S}.$$

These rules which amongst others, define the interrelationship between the growth rate, the aggregate NI/NCE and the earning power of building brick, provide interesting indications for the construction of financial growth models, and are thus of assistance in balance sheet analysis. For example if in the past the growth rate of the company has averaged say 10%, and if in that period its cash position has roughly broken even (after adding back dividends and after adding back to net income interest on loans with a corresponding correction for taxes) then its NI/NCE should be of the order of 9% and the earning power of building brick should be 10%. If on that basis the company NI/NCE has been lower than 9% from time to time, it may have been due to fluctuations in economic activity or acquisitions, or a change of depreciation policy or a combination of these factors. Again if there has been a financial deficit after the above corrections have been made, then a 10% growth rate may be accompanied by a company NI/NCE lower than 9% and the earning power of building brick would be lower than 10%. Obviously each case would have to be studied separately in the light of the available information.

However whilst these rules may be useful as a starting point, they do not provide an easy solution. The very simple formula for the company NI/NCE at the critical growth rate contains no basic data, and therefore it applies to any set of basic data which may be assumed. However the ratio applies to separate constituents of the cash flow calculation and therefore basic data can be calculated if others are known (or assumed).

Useful information can also be obtained by using such proportions as depreciation/book value because that proportion can in conjunction with the growth rate, be used to calculate, e.g., the depreciation period and the life time of building brick if C is known (see Appendix 1). Even at growth rates other than the critical growth rate, the depreciation period can be calculated because the proportion of depreciation to book value can normally be obtained from the accounts.

Nevertheless formidable difficulties remain in the construction of a financial growth model which is to represent the historical growth process of the company. A description of building brick with a given earning power can be achieved with any combination of PIP's and PAP's and therefore a *realistic* model can only be constructed if estimates have been made of, or information collected on data for building brick such as:

(1) the phasing of capital expenditure,
(2) the build-up of sales to full capacity,
(3) the build-up of stocks, debtors and other working capital,
(4) the life time of the investment over which the earning power is
    calculated and/or the   corresponding depreciation period, etc.

It may be concluded that in spite of these difficulties a useful function for the discounted cash flow remains in the construction of financial growth models, because a few simple rules apply and these are expressed in terms of discounted cash flow. They provide a reference point which is valuable although they do not by themselves give a complete solution. They are therefore a useful tool and increase the insight into the problems concerned. It may well be thought that they add a further dimension to the analysis by introducing a further parameter, i.e., that of the rate of growth.

SUMMARY

Introduction

On the face of it, there seems to be a contradiction in the widespread use of the DCF technique as a criterion for assessing the attractiveness of a project, because the success of the company in the market is measured not in terms of discounted cash flow, but in terms of net income, net income as a percentage of net capital employed, its ability to finance its own growth, its ability to pay dividends, etc.

This study attempts to analyse the problem. It is confined entirely to an analysis of the criterion itself particularly within the context of the growth of the business as a whole.

The interrelationships of cash flow, net income, net capital employed and the major profitability criteria

The interrelationships of the various major profitability criteria which are available can be summarised as follows (see also Graph S. 1):

Cash flow and net income. The aggregate of the cash flow during the life time of the project is equal to the aggregate of the net income during the same period.

Cash flow, net income and net capital employed. The cumulative net income (if it is positive) minus the cumulative cash flow, is equal to the net capital employed.

Present day value and pay-out time. There is a 50/50 chance that the criterion of PDV prefers the alternative with the longest pay-out time and therefore the later cash flow.

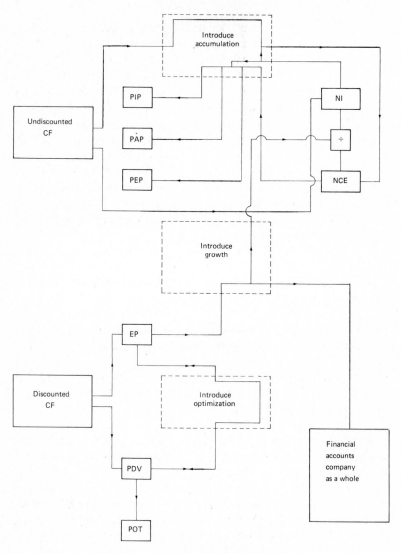

Graph S.1. A schematic representation of the relationships between the major profitability criteria.

Earning power and PDV. The investment is optimized according to the criteria of the discounted cash flow, at the point at which the marginal earning power of the alternatives is equal to the cost of capital, or at the point at which the PDV at a discount rate equal to the cost of capital, shows an optimum. The two criteria of the discounted cash flow lead to the same optimum.

Earning power and the financial position of the company as a whole. If a financial growth model of a company is described by investments each year which generate the same earning power S and which have a scale $1 + G$ as large as that in the previous year (whereby G is the rate of growth) and if $S = G$, then the financial surplus on the source and disposition of funds in the year n when the dynamic equilibrium has set in, is equal to nil.

Earning power and net income as a percentage of net capital employed. If a financial growth model of a company is described by investments each year which generate the same earning power S and which have a scale $1 + G$ as large as that in the previous year (whereby G is the rate of growth) and if $S = G$, then the net income as a percentage of the net capital employed for the company as a whole is equal to:

$$\frac{S}{1+S} \quad \text{or} \quad \frac{G}{1+G} \; .$$

Chapter 1.   A study model – procedure, definitions, etc.

An example is given of the calculation of the cash flow, earning power, present day value, net income and net capital employed of a project 'P'.

Comments are made on the various items which make up the calculation, and terms are defined.

Chapter 2.   The principle of earning power and present day value

The nature of the criteria of earning power and present day value are analysed, and it is shown that each of them can be interpreted in two different ways: the reducing balance interpretation and the compound interest interpretation. It is suggested that for earning power the reducing balance interpretation and for present day value the compound interest interpretation is the most practical.

The criterion of earning power focuses attention on only one aspect of the cost of capital, i.e., the rate of interest or discount percentage. However two further facets of the cost of capital, the length of the loan and the redemption pattern are also important but these are often ignored. It follows that earning power without specifying a corresponding life time   is meaningless. This also applies to PDV.

The criterion of PDV is very convenient to use as a selection criterion because the highest PDV of two alternatives would be the preferred choice. However there are formidable difficulties attached to its use from the point of view of time preference (see Chapter 3).

It is concluded that whilst the criteria of the discounted cash flow give an indication of the profitability of the new investment they do not reproduce the profitability results as they would actually be found in the books of the company. From that point of view they are abstract. Nor do they place the new investment against the background of the existing company. As such the criteria have limited value and are of secondary importance as profitability criteria.

Chapter 3.   Discounted cash flow and time preference

It is well known that at a given undiscounted aggregate of a cash flow the earning power of that cash is higher, the earlier is the incidence of that cash flow.

The relationship between the size of the PDV and time preference is more complicated than that. If the criterion for an early and a late cash flow is defined as the pay-out time then there is a 50/50 chance that the PDV criterion selects a late cash flow. This can be shown by distinguishing 8 cases in which the size of the undiscounted aggregate of the cash flows and the earning power of those cash flows, are the major parameters.

The conclusion is reached that if the PDV criterion is to be used at all it is also necessary to work out further profitability criteria for the two alternatives from which an advisable discount rate follows.

Chapter 4. Discounted cash flow and net income

The relationship between cash flow and net income is a relationship over time, that is to say their totals during the life time of the project are equal. This equality can only be achieved by adding back working capital at the end of the period. It means that a life time must be assigned to the project because realisation of working capital only makes sense if it is simultaneously assumed that the new investment with its attendant operations is liquidated at the end of its life. Thus the discipline of the discounted cash flow commits the evaluator to make two assumptions which it is not necessary for him to make if he uses the financial accounts profitability criteria, i.e., that the project has a life time and that all working capital is realised at the end of it. Therefore the advantage which is often claimed for the discounted cash flow, that it can be calculated without using book entries (except for the tax calculation) is replaced by two greater disadvantages: that the evaluator may have to make an assumption on the realisation of working capital which may be at variance with his own expectations, and that he has to make an assumption on life time which he may not be able or willing to make.

The treatment of fixed investment and working capital by the discounted cash flow causes there to be a divergency between the time profile of net income, and that of the corresponding cash flow. As a result a given earning power does not represent a unique result in the books of the company because a given earning power may be associated with a different NI/NCE in individual years according to the proportion of fixed investment to working capital in the original investment. With a given NI/NCE in individual years the earning power is higher, the higher is the proportion of working capital to fixed investment.

Examples which are all based on the actual experience of the author, illustrate that earning power may be an unreliable guide to profitability in accounting terms. The one figure of earning power which summarises a profitability over a number of years may conceal figures in individual years which may be of vital importance to the prosperity of the company.

Chapter 5.   Present day value as a selection criterion for mutually exclusive projects

The PDV criterion is convenient to use for selection purposes because in contrast to the financial accounts profitability criterion, it sum- marises profitability in one figure. However the relationship between the timing of the cash flow and the size of the PDV may seriously af- fect the soundness of the decision because blind and exclusive use of the PDV criterion may result in the project with the longest pay-out time being selected. This is particularly important in cases which by their very nature imply a choice between an early and a late cash flow because that would be a major aspect of the problem on which the management would have to take a decision. Examples of this are a choice between manufacturing a product or buying it in, or the selec- tion of the capacity of a plant. Cases from the actual experience of the author show that the comparative size of the PDV's of the two alter- natives is very sensitive to the discount rate, which itself is selected with a considerable degree of arbitrariness. Consequently the level of the discount rate may be decisive for the choice, and all relevant facts which should be the basis for the decision do not come to the surface.

Similar problems arise if the investment is optimised by, e.g., op- timisation of capacity. Optimisation occurs if the marginal earning power of the stepwise increases in capacity is equal to the cost of capital, or if the PDV at a discount rate which is equal to the cost of capital, is optimised. From an example inspired by the actual ex- perience of the author it is shown that of the 13 steps in capacity in- creases towards the optimum, 9 steps are from an early cash flow to a late cash flow and 4 steps from a late cash flow to an early cash flow.

The example demonstrates that for many reasons the technique of optimising the investment by the criterion of the discounted cash flow has little useful value. A logical case is made for very different optima if other major criteria such as POT and those of the financial accounts are used. However there is not really an objective function for optimising any investment and direct judgment should also be brought to bear on it.

Chapter 6. *Discounted cash flow and growth of the business*

A new investment has a depressing effect on the profitability of the company as a whole because of the following reasons:

(1) The capital which is locked up in partially completed plant during the building period yields no return until production (and sales) begin, and only add to the net capital employed.
(2) The new plant incurs pre-operational expenses.
(3) The new plant does not operate at full capacity until a number of years after it has started operations.
(4) The book value of plant is higher in the initial years than in the later years.
(5) If an existing business is taken over, the various functions (such as production, marketing, etc.) have to be integrated with those of the existing company; this entails costs.
(6) Interest on loans is higher in the early years than in the later years because loans are reduced as and when the new investment generates cash to repay the loan.

Cases may also occur in which the net income of the new investment is high in the initial years and lower in later years. This may mitigate the depressing effect of the new investment although it does not eradicate it.

The principles involved can be illustrated by a simple growth model. From the analysis it follows that financial results generated by a new investment in the early years should not be given more or less weight than those generated in the later years as the criteria of the discounted cash flow with their time preference do; for earning power overemphasises the early years and underemphasises the later years, and PDV may do the opposite. Yet within the context of growth both the initial period and the later period should be studied.

The growth model illustrates that the cash flow of the company as a whole is composed of the cash flows of the individual projects each in their own state of development in that particular year. The cash flow of the new investment should therefore be related to that of the existing business. The discounted cash flow ignores this, because it studies the new investment in isolation, 'an' investment.

It follows that within that context there is no room for the 'cost of capital' as handled by the discounted cash flow, because discounted cash flow assesses the investment in isolation whereas the company faces the realities of the financial world not on the level of the individual project, but on a broader level that of the company as a whole. The problem of the cost of capital arises not only in connection with the earning power of the individual projects which together constitute the company, but also in connection with the rate of growth of the company.

Chapter 7.   *An alternative suggestion – The PIP, PAP and PEP*

The influence which any new investment has on the overall profitability of the company varies from case to case, and depends not only on the nature and profitability of that investment, but also on its size in relation to the existing business, and the profitability of the existing business itself. In order to take all factors into account, the new investment should be 'grafted' on to the existing business, and the financial results of the company as a whole with and without the new investment should then be compared.

This procedure is very cumbersome. Therefore a shorthand for the profitability of the new investment is suggested. The criteria attach equal weight to the profitability in the initial and later years. They are:

(1)   PIP – Profitability in the Initial Period,
(2)   PAP – Profitability After the initial Period,
(3)   PEP – Profitability in the Entire Period.

The PIP is defined as the weighted average of the NI/NCE (expressed as a %) during the period which commences when the first money/capital on the project is spent, and terminates a number of years (p years) after the new project has come into operation.

The PAP is defined as the weighted average of the NI/NCE during a period of q years which commences in year $p + 1$ and terminates q years thereafter.

The PEP is defined as the weighted average of NI/NCE during the entire period from the year in which the first money/capital on the project is spent to the last operating year.

The PIP, PAP and PEP are in no way related to the cost of capital. Their desirable levels, their desirable relative size, and the appropriate number of years for p and q, vary widely between individual industries because they reflect divergencies of economic structure. A cut-off point for the PIP and PAP can only be given if a rhythmical growth pattern of the business can be discerned and if the investment steps in that business can be fitted into one or more categories each with their own financial structure. Desirable levels of the PIP and PAP can then be defined. If this is not possible, then every new investment should be looked at separately against the background of the overall profitability.

In practice the investment plans of the company can be kept under review by keeping on a routine basis a simple list – the Profitability And Investment List, the PAIL. It shows the capital expenditure, net income and losses generated by the new investments against the background of those of the existing business and the objectives set by the management, and the source and disposition of funds of the business as a whole. An analysis of a fictitious investment plan is given, and the merits of cancellations or postponements of individual items is discussed.

Chapter 8.   Earning power and financial growth models

Further study of the financial growth model presented in Chapter 6 shows that there is a useful relationship between the discounted cash flow and the financial accounts if the rate of growth is introduced as a further parameter. Some simple rules apply. They are expressed in terms of earning power, and they provide a reference point in balance sheet analysis. They can be summarised as follows:

If the earning power of 'building brick' and subsequent investments is equal to the growth rate, then the company as a whole breaks even on the source and disposition of funds. At that point the aggregate NI/NCE is equal to:

$$\frac{S}{1+S} \quad \text{or} \quad \frac{G}{1+G},$$

where S is the earning power, G is the growth rate, and $S = G$. This growth rate has been called the critical growth rate.

At growth rates other than the critical growth rate, earning power by itself inadequately defines building brick, because the company NI/NCE is determined not only by earning power but also by the PIP, PAP and PEP at that earning power (and that growth rate). A given earning power can be achieved with any combination of PIP's and PAP's.

The company NI/NCE falls as the rate of growth increases. It is also more sensitive to growth at a low PIP and correspondingly high PAP than at a high PIP and a correspondingly low PAP. It is also more sensitive to growth at a high earning power of building brick and subsequent investments than at a low earning power.

At low growth rates and at a given earning power of building brick and subsequent investments, a high PIP and a correspondingly low PAP produce a higher company NI/NCE than a low PIP and a correspondingly high PAP. At high growth rates the reverse is true. Between these limits there is a growth rate – the critical growth rate – at which the company NI/NCE is independent of the PIP, PAP and PEP and also of the depreciation period.

The construction of a financial growth model along these lines adds a further dimension to balance sheet analysis by adding one more parameter, i.e., that of the rate of growth.

CONCLUSIONS

The DCF technique is considered to be by itself a questionable criterion for assessing the profitability of a new investment because of the following reasons:

(1) It misses the plain logic that if a company wants to achieve an acceptable net income for the business as a whole, net income for the new investment should be worked out and studied. Equally if the company wants to achieve an acceptable NI/NCE it should be worked out and studied for the new investment. Discounted cash flow does not reproduce the profitability results as they are recorded in the books of the company. Therefore it is abstract.

(2) It considers the new investment in isolation, as 'an' investment without it being placed against the background of the company as a whole. Thus a given profitability is attractive or unattractive irrespective of the fact whether the business as a whole is in a healthy state or not.

(3) It is inherent in the DCF technique that figures for individual years are summarised into one figure. Therefore the method does not allow the financial results of individual years to be highlighted. There may be circumstances in which this is highly desirable 'because it is no good being rich in the long run if the business goes bankrupt in the short run'.

(4) The criterion of present day value may reverse time preference, i.e., a high positive PDV may be associated with a high earning power (which is favourable) but also with a late cash flow (which is unfavourable). By contrast the criterion of earning power favours an early cash flow. The PDV criterion may give preference to an irrational solution in mutually exclusive projects.

(5) The DCF technique commits the evaluator to an assumption which he may not be prepared to make, i.e., that all working

capital is cashed in at the end of the period, and at its historical cost/value. Thus the advantage which is often claimed for the discounted cash flow that it circumvents the use of book entries (i.e., depreciation) is replaced by two greater disadvantages: that it commits the evaluator to make an assumption on working capital which may be at variance with his own expectations, and that it commits the evaluator to make an assumption on the life time of the project which is not directly essential for the evaluation and can be avoided if other methods are used.

(6) The treatment of working capital by the discounted cash flow causes there to be a distortion in the time profile of the data which are assessed in the DCF technique (i.e., cash flow), and that of the data by which the company is directly assessed in the market, i.e., net income and net income as a percentage of net capital employed. This means that an acceptable earning power does not necessarily mean an acceptable profitability in terms of the financial accounts. Furthermore a given earning power does not represent a unique financial result in the books of the company because the interrelationship between earning power and profitability in accounting terms depends on the proportion of fixed investment to working capital in the initial outlay of the new investment.

(7) The optimisation of a proposed investment in terms of the discounted cash flow, by working out a solution whereby the marginal earning power is equal to the assumed cost of capital, or the PDV is an optimum at that cost of capital (discount rate), which takes the theory to its logical conclusion, may result in solutions which are unacceptable to sound judgment and common sense, e.g., too big a plant may result from the optimisation. Furthermore if costs per unit of product are higher, the discounted cash flow recommends a smaller plant thus aggravating the consequences, because with a given demand pattern a smaller plant would create a need to build additional capacity sooner and a costlier solution in time would follow. This again is contrary to sound judgment.

(8) The concept of the cost of capital as handled by the discounted

cash flow, applies to the individual project, whereas the company faces the problem of the finance of the company on a corporate level. Not only the earning power of the individual investments but also the rate of growth determines what cost of capital the company as a whole can carry.

(9) The theory of the discounted cash flow conceals two very important facets of the cost of capital, i.e., the length of the loan and the redemption pattern. A blind use of the discounted cash flow which normally handles a percentage only to express the cost of capital, may lead to a direct comparison of cases which are in fact not comparable.

(10) Within the context of growth the financial results generated by a new investment in the early years should not be given more or less weight than those generated in the later years as the criteria of the discounted cash flow with their time preference do. Equal weight should be attached to either period because the financial results in each of them play their own (and divergent) role in the growth process. They should therefore be studied separately and each in their own right.

The ultimate criterion for the profitability of a new investment can only be the influence of the new investment on the financial accounts of the company, because the quality of the financial accounts determines the ability of the company to attract further finance, and its ability to survive. The purpose of project evaluation is therefore 'to assemble basic data, carry out calculations and assess the resulting figures, with a view to investigating what differences over a period of years, the new project will make to the financial accounts of the company'.

It follows that there is a need for a clear understanding of the way in which the new investment influences the overall financial accounts. In that connection two distinct periods should be distinguished in the life time of the new investment. In each of these periods the new investment plays a very different role in the growth process of the company.

Period 1:   The period in which the new investment constitutes a burden to the overall results – the Initial Period. The profitability during this period which has been called the PIP, quantifies this burden.

Period 2:   The period in which the new project has a high profitability in terms of net income/net capital employed, well above that of the business as a whole. This enables the project to support the burdens of further new investments without the profitability of the entire business falling to an unacceptable level. The profitability in this period is the Profitability After the initial Period (the PAP), and quantifies this 'upholding' ability.

The desirable profitability level during the two periods should reflect the structure of the individual business, and therefore no definition of the length of the periods or the cut off points can be given which is universally valid for all industry. In other words each business and/or industry has to be studied separately in the light of its own problems. Furthermore a desirable PIP and PAP level can only be defined if a rhythmical pattern in the growth of the business can be discerned.

In spite of the fact that the PIP and PAP have been designed to study the new investment against the background of the existing business there remains the need to 'graft' the new investments periodically onto the accounts of the existing business so as to ensure that the adopted growth rate is not too heavy a burden for the company. A simple list, the 'Profitability And Investment List' (the PAIL) which lists on a routine basis the planned new investments together with the profits and/or losses they generate, is suggested as an instrument to keep the investment plans under constant review.

There are two very useful relationships between the discounted cash flow and the financial accounts. This is of importance in the building of financial growth models. It adds a further dimension to balance sheet analysis by taking into account the rate of growth. The PIP, PAP and PEP are indispensable aids in the analysis.

APPENDIX 1

The relationship between the discounted cash flow,
the rate of growth, and the NI/NCE

The following symbols have been used:

m	– the number of pre-operational years of building brick and subsequent investments;
n	– the life time (in years) of building brick and subsequent investments from the first building year to the last operating year;
$a_1, a_2, \ldots, a_m$	– additions to capital expenditure of building brick in years 1, 2, .., m;
C	– total capital expenditure on completed plant of building brick;
$W_1, W_2, \ldots, W_m$	– increases in working capital of building bricks in years 1, 2, ..., m;
W	– the total working capital of building brick;
S	– the earning power of building brick and subsequent investments (as a fraction);
G	– the growth rate (as a fraction);
$A_1, A_2, \ldots, A_n$	– the cash generation of building brick in years $m + 1$, $m + 2$, ..., $n - 1$, n;

All financial quantities are expressed in FU's.

If it is assumed that there is no working capital, then the cash flow of building brick is calculated as follows:

Year	Cash gen.	Capital exp.	Cash flow
1		$-a_1$	$-a_1$
2		$-a_2$	$-a_2$
.		.	.
.		.	.
.		.	.
		$-a_m$	$-a_m$
$m+1$	A_1	$(C - a_1 - \cdots - a_m)$	$(A_1 - C + a_1 + \cdots + a_m)$
.	.		.
.	.		.
$n-1$	A_{n-1}		A_{n-1}
n	A_n		A_n

If the earning power of this cash flow is equal to S, then the discounted aggregate is equal to zero:

Year	DCF
1	$-a_1$
2	$-\dfrac{a_2}{(1+S)}$
.	.
.	.
m	$\dfrac{a_m}{(1+S)^{m-1}}$
$m+1$	$\dfrac{A_1 - C + a_1 + a_2 + \cdots + a_m}{(1+S)^m}$

$\vdots$

$$n-1 \qquad\qquad \frac{A_{n-1}}{(1+S)^{n-2}}$$

$$n \qquad\qquad \frac{A_n}{(1+S)^{n-1}}$$

$$\sum = 0$$

This equation can be restated by multiplying by $(1+S)^{n-1}$ and separating the terms with $A_1, \ldots, A_{n-1}, A_n$ from the remaining ones:

(1)	(2)
$A_1 (1+S)^{n-m-1}$	$a_1 (1+S)^{n-1}$
$\vdots$	$\vdots$
$+A_{n-1}(1+S)$	$a_m (1+S)^{n-m}$
$+A_n$	$C (1+S)^{n-m-1}$
	$-a_1 (1+S)^{n-m-1}$
	$-a_2 (1+S)^{n-m-1}$
	$\vdots$
	$-a_m(1+S)^{n-m-1}$
$\sum (1)$	$\sum (2)$

$$\sum (1) = \sum (2)$$

This is equation 1.

The net income of building brick is calculated as follows:

Year	Cash gen.	Dep.	NI
$m+1$	A_1	$\dfrac{C}{n-m}$	$A_1 - \dfrac{C}{n-m}$
$\vdots$	$\vdots$	$\vdots$	$\vdots$
$n-1$	A_{n-1}	$\dfrac{C}{n-m}$	$A_{n-1} - \dfrac{C}{n-m}$
n	A_n	$\dfrac{C}{n-m}$	$A_n - \dfrac{C}{n-m}$

If it is assumed that the growth rate is equal to G, then the aggregate net income in year n is:

$$A_1(1+G)^{n-m-1} - \frac{C}{n-m}(1+G)^{n-m-1}$$

$$\vdots$$

$$A_{n-1}(1+G) - \frac{C}{n-m}(1+G)$$

$$A_n - \frac{C}{n-m}$$

$$\sum = \text{Aggregate NI in year } n$$

This is equation 2.

If $S = G$ and if the value for:

$$A_1(1+S)^{n-m-1}$$
$$\vdots$$
$$+ A_{n-1}(1+S)$$
$$+ A_n$$

of equation 1 is substituted in equation 2, then the aggregate net income in year n is:

$$a_1 (1 + G)^{n-1}$$
$$+ a_2 (1 + G)^{n-2}$$
$$\cdot$$
$$\cdot$$
$$\cdot$$
$$+ a_m (1 + G)^{n-m}$$
$$- a_1 (1 + G)^{n-m-1}$$
$$- a_2 (1 + G)^{n-m-1}$$
$$\cdot$$
$$\cdot$$
$$\cdot$$
$$- a_m (1 + G)^{n-m-1}$$
$$+ C (1 + G)^{n-m-1}$$
$$- \frac{C}{n - m}(1 + G)^{n-m-1}$$
$$\cdot$$
$$\cdot$$
$$\cdot$$
$$- \frac{C}{n - m}(1 + G)$$
$$- \frac{C}{n - m}$$

$$\overline{\sum = \text{Aggregate NI in year } n}$$

This is equation 3.

It consists of two main parts:
(1) the phasing of the capital expenditure in the pre-operational years – the terms with $a_1, a_2, \ldots, a_m$;
(2) the total capital expenditure and depreciation – the terms with C. Each part will be considered separately in the light of the corresponding net capital employed.

The net capital employed of building brick, in so far as the portions of capital expenditure $(a_1, a_2, ..., a_m)$ are concerned is:

Year	NCE
1	a_1
2	$a_1 + a_2$
.	.
.	.
.	.
m	$a_1 + a_2 + ... + a_m$

The corresponding items which go into the aggregate net capital employed in year n are:

$$a_1 (1 + G)^{n-1}$$
$$(a_1 + a_2) (1 + G)^{n-2}$$
$$.$$
$$.$$
$$.$$
$$(a_1 + a_2 + ... + a_m)(1 + G)^{n-m}$$

$\sum$ = Aggregate NCE for these items in year n

This is equation 4.

The ratio of $G/(1 + G) = S/(1 + S)$ applies separately to each of the items $a_1, a_2, ..., a_m$, as they appear in equation 3 and equation 4. For instance take portion a_1:

As in equation 3 (1)	As in equation 4 (2)
$a_1 (1 + G)^{n-1}$ $- a_1 (1 + G)^{n-m-1}$	$a_1 (1 + G)^{n-1}$ $+ a_1 (1 + G)^{n-2}$ $+ a_1 (1 + G)^{n-m}$

$$\sum(1) = (1 + G)^{n-1} \, a_1 \{ 1 - (1 + G)^{-m} \}$$

$$\sum(2) = (1 + G)^{n-1} \, a_1 \left\{ \frac{1 - (1 + G)^{-m}}{1 - (1 + G)^{-1}} \right\}$$

It follows that $\sum(1) \div \sum(2)$ is equal to:

$$\frac{G}{1 + G} = \frac{S}{1 + S} \; .$$

Or take a portion a_m:

As in equation 3 (1)	As in equation 4 (2)
$a_m (1 + G)^{n-m}$ $- a_m (1 + G)^{n-m-1}$	$a_m (1 + G)^{n-m}$
$\sum(1) = a_m (1 + G)^{n-m}$ $- a_m (1 + G)^{n-m-1}$	$\sum(2) = a_m (1 + G)^{n-m}$

It follows that $\sum(1) \div \sum(2)$ is equal to:

$$\frac{G}{1 + G} = \frac{S}{1 + S} \; .$$

The aggregate depreciation in year n as shown in equation 3 is as follows:

$$\frac{C}{n - m} \, (1 + G)^{n-m-1}$$
$$\vdots$$
$$\frac{C}{n - m} \, (1 + G)$$
$$\frac{C}{n - m}$$

There are $n - m$ operating years and each investment is written off in $n - m$ years. The aggregate depreciation in year n expressed as a general formula is:

$$\frac{C}{n - m} \times (1 + G)^{n-m-1} \left\{ \frac{1 - \dfrac{1}{(1 + G)^{n - m}}}{1 - \dfrac{1}{(1 + G)}} \right\}.$$

This is equation 5.

The book value of building brick is as follows:

Year	Book value
$m + 1$	$C - \dfrac{C}{n - m}$
.	.
.	.
$n + 1$	$C - \dfrac{(n - m - 1)\,C}{n - m}$
n	$C - \dfrac{(n - m)\,C}{n - m}$

The aggregate book value in year n is:

$$\left\{ C - \frac{C}{n - m} \right\} (1 + G)^{n-m-1}$$

$$\vdots$$

$$\left\{ C - \frac{(n - m - 1)\,C}{n - m} \right\} (1 + G)$$

$$C - \frac{(n - m)\,C}{n - m}$$

_____

$\sum$ = aggregate book value in year n

In general the aggregate book value in year n is:

$$\frac{C}{n-m} \times \frac{(1+G)^{n-m}}{G}$$

$$\times \left\{ (n-m-1) - \frac{(1+G)^{n-m-1}-1}{G(1+G)^{n-m-1}} \right\}.$$

This is equation 6.

The equation is not immediately clear. It can be tested as follows: If it is assumed that $C = 1000$, $n = 6$, $m = 2$ and $G = 0.1$, then the aggregate book value in year n is:

$$\frac{1000}{6-2} \times \frac{1.1^4}{0.1} \left\{ (6-2-1)' - \frac{1.1^{6-2-1}-1}{(0.1)(1.1)^{6-2-1}} \right\}$$

$$= 3660 \left\{ 3 - \frac{0.331}{0.1 \times 1.331} \right\} = 1878.$$

The aggregate book value in year n can also be calculated as follows: the book value of building brick in each of the years 3, 4, 5 and 6 is:

Year	Book value
3	750
4	500
5	250
6	0

The aggregate book value in year 6 is:

$$750 \times (1.1)^3 = 998$$
$$500 \times (1.1)^2 = 605$$

$$250 \times (1.1) = 275$$
$$0 = 0$$

$$\overline{}$$
$$1878$$

This agrees with the total as calculated by using equation 6.

The ratio can now be calculated, and the term $C(1 + G)^{n-m-1}$ of equation 1 should also be included. The ratio is equal to:

$$\frac{C(1 + G)^{n-m-1} - \text{Aggregate depreciation}}{\text{Aggregate book value}}.$$

In the example:

$$\frac{1331 - 1160}{1878} = \frac{171}{1878} = 0.09 = \frac{G}{1 + G} = \frac{S}{1 + S}.$$

In general the ratio can be shown to apply as follows: subtracting the aggregate depreciation equation 5 from:

$$C(1 + G)^{n-m-1}$$

yields:

$$C(1 + G)^{n-m-1} - \frac{C}{n - m}(1 + G)^{n-m-1}\left\{ \frac{1 - \dfrac{1}{(1 + G)^{n-m}}}{1 - \dfrac{1}{1 + G}} \right\}.$$

Dividing by C this can be restated to read:

$$(1 + G)^{n-m-1} - \frac{1}{n - m} \times \frac{1 + G}{G} \times (1 + G)^{n-m-1} + \frac{1}{n - m} \times \frac{1}{1 + G} \times \frac{1 + G}{G}.$$

This is equation 7.

Equation 6 for the aggregate book value namely:

$$\frac{C}{n-m} \times \frac{(1+G)^{n-m}}{G} \left\{ (n-m-1) - \frac{(1+G)^{n-m-1}-1}{G(1+G)^{n-m-1}} \right\}$$

can be restated to read (after dividing by C):

$$\frac{(1+G)^{n-m}}{G} - \frac{(1+G)^{n-m}}{G(n-m)} - \frac{(1+G)^{n-m}}{G^2(n-m)} + \frac{1+G}{G^2(n-m)} \;,$$

or:

$$\frac{1+G}{G} \left\{ (1+G)^{n-m-1} - \frac{(1+G)^{n-m-1}}{n-m} - \frac{(1+G)^{n-m-1}}{G(n-m)} + \frac{1}{G(n-m)} \right\}$$

or:

$$\frac{1+G}{G} \left\{ (1+G)^{n-m-1} - \frac{1}{n-m} \times \frac{1+G}{G} \times (1+G)^{n-m-1} + \frac{1}{G(n-m)} \right\}$$

This is equation 8.

It follows that the ratio between equation 7 and equation 8 is equal to:

$$\frac{G}{1+G} = \frac{S}{1+S} \;.$$

It remains to introduce working capital into the analysis. If it is assumed that there is no fixed investment, but only working capital, then the cash flow of building brick is calculated as follows:

Year	Cash gen.	Working capital	Cash flow
1		W_m	$-W_1$
2		W_2	$-W_2$
.		.	.
.		.	.
.		.	.
m		W_m	$-W_m$
$m+1$	A_1	$W-W_1-\cdots-W_m$	$A_1-W+W_1+\cdots+W_m$
.	.		.
.	.		.
.	.		.
$n-1$	A_{n-1}		A_{n-1}
n	A_n		A_n
		Value under Res.	W

If the earning power of the cash flow is equal to S, then the discounted aggregate is equal to 0:

$$-W_1$$

$$-\frac{W_2}{1+S}$$

$$\vdots$$

$$-\frac{W_m}{(1+S)^{m-1}}$$

$$\frac{A_1-W+W_1+W_2+\ldots+W_m}{(1+S)^m}$$

$$\vdots$$

$$\frac{A_{n-1}}{(1+S)^{n-2}}$$

$$\frac{A_n}{(1+S)^{n-1}} + \frac{W}{(1+S)^{n-1}}$$

$$\sum = 0$$

After multiplying by $(1+S)^{n-1}$, and separating the cash generation from the working capital, this can be restated to read:

(1)	(2)
$A_1(1+S)^{n-m-1}$	$W_1(1+S)^{n-1}$
$\vdots$	$W_2(1+S)^{n-2}$
$A_n(1+S)$	$\vdots$
	$W_m(1+S)^{n-m}$
A_n	$(W-W_1-W_m)(1+S)^{n-m-1}$
	$-W$
$\sum(1)$	$\sum(2)$

$$\sum(1) = \sum(2)$$

This is equation 9.

If it is assumed that the growth rate equals G then the aggregate net income in year n is:

$$A_1(1 + G)^{n-m-1}$$

$$\vdots$$

$$+ A_{n-1}(1 + G)$$
$$+ A_n$$

$$\sum = \text{Aggregate NI in year } n$$

This·is equation 10.

If it is further assumed that $S = G$, it follows from equations 9 and 10 that the aggregate net income in year n is equal to:

$$W_1 (1 + G)^{n-1}$$
$$\vdots$$
$$+ W_m (1 + G)^{n-m}$$
$$+ W (1 + G)^{n-m-1}$$
$$- W_1 (1 + G)^{n-m-1}$$
$$\vdots$$
$$- W_m (1 + G)^{n-m-1}$$
$$- W$$

$$\sum = \text{Aggregate NI in year } n$$

This is equation 11.

The net capital employed of building brick is as follows:

Year	NCE
1	W_1
2	$W_1 + W_2$
$\vdots$	$\vdots$

m	$W_1 + W_2 + \ldots + W_m$
$m + 1$	W
$\vdots$	$\vdots$
$n - 1$	W
n	$W - W$

The aggregate NCE in year n assuming a growth rate of G is:

$$W_1 (1 + G)^{n-1}$$
$$+ (W_1 + W_2)(1 + G)^{n-2}$$
$$\vdots$$
$$+ (W_1 + W_2 + \ldots + W_m)(1 + G)^{n-m}$$
$$+ W(1 + G)^{n-m-1}$$
$$\vdots$$
$$+ W(1 + G)$$
$$+ W - W$$

$$\overline{\sum = \text{Aggregate NCE in year } n}$$

This is equation 12.

The ratio holds good for all portions of $W_1, W_2, \ldots, W_m$ and W as they appear in equation 11 and equation 12. Take portion W_1:·

As in equation 11
(1)

$$W_1 (1 + G)^{n-1}$$
$$-W_1 (1 + G)^{n-m-1}$$

$$\sum (1) = W_1 (1 + G)^{n-1} \{ 1-(1 + G)^{-m} \}$$

As in equation 12
(2)

$$W_1 (1 + G)^{n-1}$$
$$+W_1 (1 + G)^{n-2}$$

$$\vdots$$

$$+W_1(1+G)^{n-m}$$

$$\sum(2)=(1+G)^{n-1}\left\{\frac{1-(1+G)^{-m}}{1-(1+G)^{-1}}\right\}W_1$$

$$=W_1(1+G)^{n-1}\{1-(1+G)^{-m}\}\frac{(1+G)}{G}$$

It follows that $\sum(1):\sum(2)$ is equal to:

$$\frac{G}{1+G}=\frac{S}{1+S}\ .$$

The same ratio applies to, e.g., portion W_m:

As in equation 11 (1)	As in equation 12 (2)
$W_m(1+G)^{n-m}$	$W_m(1+G)^{n-m}$
$-\,W_m(1+G)^{n-m-1}$	
$\sum(1)=W_m(1+G)^{n-m}\,\dfrac{G}{1+G}$	$\sum(2)=W_m(1+G)^{n-m}$

It follows again that $\sum(1)\div\sum(2)$ is equal to:

$$\frac{G}{1+G}=\frac{S}{1+S}\ .$$

Now take portion W:

As in equation 11

$$\frac{(1)}{W(1+G)^{n-m-1}}$$

$$-W$$

$$\sum(1) = W(1+G)^{n-m-1} - W$$

$$= W\{(1+G)^{n-m-1} - 1\}$$

As in equation 12

$$(2)$$

$$W(1+G)^{n+m+1}$$

$$\vdots$$

$$+ W(1+G)$$

$$+ W - W$$

$$\sum(2) = W\left\{\frac{1-(1+G)^{-n+m+1}}{1-(1+G)^{-1}}\right\}(1+G)^{n-m-1}$$

$$= W(1+G)^{n-m-1}\left\{\frac{(1+G)^{n-m-1}-1}{(1+G)^{n-m-1}}\right\}\frac{1+G}{G}$$

It follows again that the ratio between $\sum(1)$ and $\sum(2)$ is equal to:

$$\frac{G}{1+G} = \frac{S}{1+S}.$$

It has been shown that this ratio applies to all components of a cash flow, profit and loss account and net capital employed calculation. Therefore it is generally valid for the financial accounts.

BIBLIOGRAPHY

Alfred, A.M., Discounted cash flow and corporate planning, Woolwich Polytechnic, Department of Economics and Business Studies, Woolwich Economic Papers No. 3, 2nd ed., 1969.

Alfred, A.M. and J.B. Evans, Appraisal of investment projects by discounted cash flow, Principles and some short cut techniques, 3rd ed., Chapman and Hall, 1971.

Aydin, Cyril, Financing your company: a critical guide, Management Publications, London, 1972.

Baldwin, R., How to assess investment proposals, Harvard Business Review, May–June 1959, page 98.

Bond, G.D., Corporate finance for management, Butterworths, London, 1974.

Bradley, Joseph F., Administrative financial management, 2nd ed., Holt, Rinehart and Winston, New York, 1969.

Brandt, Louis K., Analysis for financial management, Prentice Hall, Englewood Cliffs, N.J., 1972.

Cherry, Richard T., Introduction to business finance, Wadsworth Publishing Co., Belmont, California, 1970.

Curran, Ward S., Principles of financial management, McGraw-Hill, New York, 1970.

Donaldson, Elvin F. and John K. Pfahl, Corporate finance, Policy and management, 3rd ed., The Ronald Press, New York, 1969.

Drew, Carran R., Financing business and industry, Pan Books Ltd. and David and Charles Ltd., Newton Abbot, 1971.

European Chemical News, Assessing a project, 14th February 1964 (page 28) and 28th February 1964 (page 29).

Financial Management Handbook, Gower Press, Epping, 1972.

Freear, John, Financing decisions in business, Accountancy Age Books, Haymarket Publishing Ltd., London, 1973.

Grunenwald, Adolph E. and Erwin Esser Nemmers, Basic managerial finance, Holt, Rinehart and Winston, New York, 1970.

Harvard Business Review, Finance Series, Reprints from the Harvard Business Review, Harvard, 1964–1967.

Harvard Business Review, Capital investment series, Part II, Reprints from Harvard Business Review, Harvard, 1965–1969.

Hastings, Paul G., The management of business finance, Van Nostrand Company, Princeton, 1966.

Heukensfeldt Jansen, H.P.J., The DCF technique as a criterion for project evaluation, and: Project evaluation and growth of the company, Economisch-Statistische Berichten, resp. 29th March 1967 (page 343) and 5th April 1967 (page 362) (in Dutch).

Imperial Chemical Industries, Assessing projects, Methuen, London, 1974.

Johnson, Robert W., Financial management, 3rd ed., Allyn and Bacon Inc., Boston, Mass., 1966.

Lerner, Eugene M. and Alfred Rappaport, Limit DCF in capital budgeting, Harvard Business Review, Sept./Oct., 1968, page 133.

Lerner, Eugene M., Managerial finance, Harcourt Brace Jovanovich, New York, 1971.

Lindsay, J. Robert and Arnold W. Sametz, Financial management, An analytical approach, Richard D. Irwin, Homewood, Illinois, 1967.

Merrett, A.J. and Allen Sykes, The finance and analysis of capital projects, 2nd ed., Longman, 1973.

Midgeley, K. and R.G. Burns, Business finance and the capital market, Macmillan, London, 1969.

Modern Financial Management, Selected readings, Edited by B.V. Carsberg and H.C. Edey, Penguin Modern Management Readings, 1969.

Mulder, K.J., Management considerations in investment policy in industry, Stenfert Kroese, Leiden, 1967 (in Dutch).

National Economic Development Council, Investment appraisal, 2nd ed., Her Majesty's Stationery Office, 1965.

Osborn, Richard C., Business finance, The management approach, Appleton Century Crofts, New York, 1965.

Ravenscroft, Edward A., Return on investment: fit the method to your need, Harvard Business Review, March/April, 1960, page 97.

Readings in financial management, Edited by Edward J. Mock, International Textbook Company, Scranton, Penn., 1964.

Rees, R., The economics of investment analysis, Civil Service College Occasional Papers, Her Majesty's Stationery Office, London, 1973.

Robichek, Alexander A. and Stewart C. Myers, Optimal financing decisions, Prentice Hall, Englewood Cliffs, N.J., 1965.

Willems, H., The financial structure and the cost of capital in investment plans, and the cost calculations, Stenfert Kroese, Leiden, 1965 (in Dutch).

Wright, M.G., Discounted cash flow, McGraw-Hill, New York, 1967.

GLOSSARY OF ABBREVIATIONS, SYMBOLS AND TECHNICAL TERMS

$A_1, A_2, \ldots, A_n$ Mathematical symbols for the cash generation of a new investment in the first, second, etc. operational year, i.e., in years $m+1$, $m+2$, $\ldots$, n.

$a_1, a_2, \ldots, a_m$ Mathematical symbols for additions to capital expenditure in years $1, 2, \ldots, m$.

Alt. Abbreviation for alternative.

B Mathematical symbol for the aggregate book value of a financial growth model.

Building brick The initial project of a financial growth model. Any subsequent projects have the same structure and earning power as building brick, and a scale $1 + G$ as large as the investment in the previous year.

C Mathematical symbol for the total capital expenditure on a new project.

Cap. exp. Abbreviation for capital expenditure.

Cash flow Cash generation minus any expenditure on fixed investment and working capital in the appropriate year, plus (at the end of the life time of the project) the recovery of land and working capital.

Cash gen. Cash generation – cash before tax minus tax.

CBT Abbreviation for cash before tax.

CF Abbreviation for cash flow.

Cum. Abbreviation for cumulative.

D Mathematical symbol for the earning power of a differential cash flow.

Dep.   Mathematical symbol for the aggregate depreciation of a financial growth model.

DCF   Abbreviation for discounted cash flow.

Diff.   Abbreviation for differential.

DOC   Abbreviation for date of completion.

E Mathematical symbol for the earning power of an early cash flow.

Earning power   The discount rate at which the aggregate of the present day values of each of the annual cash flows, is equal to 0.

ECF   Abbreviation for early cash flow.

EP   Abbreviation for earning power.

$F_1, F_2, \ldots, F_n$ Mathematical symbols for cash flow in operating years $1, 2, \ldots, n$, generated by an investment I in year 1.

Fin. acc.   Abbreviation for financial accounts.

Financial accounts profitability criteria   Net income and net income as a percentage of net capital employed.

Financial unit   The monetary unit which has been used throughout the book. It has been assumed that it is not subject to changes in value.

FU   Abbreviation for financial unit.

G Mathematical symbol for growth rate (as a fraction).

GR   Abbreviation for growth rate.

Int.   Abbreviation for interest.

Inv.   Abbreviation for investment.

L Mathematical symbol for the earning power of a late cash flow.

LCF   Abbreviation for late cash flow.

m Mathematical symbol for the number of pre-operational years of building brick.

n Mathematical symbol for the life time of the project.

NCE   Abbreviation for net capital employed.

Neg.   Abbreviation for negative.

Netback   Net proceeds ex plant after deducting all sales expenses, commissions, sales margins, transport costs, duties, turnover taxes, etc. It is assumed that all sales are made ex plant.

Net capital employed Book value plus cumulative working capital plus cumulative losses.

NI   Abbreviation for net income.

NI/NCE   Abbreviation for net income as a percentage of net capital employed.

PAIL   Abbreviation for Profitability And Investment List.

PAP   Abbreviation for Profitability After the initial Period. It is defined as the weighted average of the net income as a percentage of the net capital employed during the period which commences in operating year $p + 1$ and terminates q years thereafter; p and q can be taken as any number of years according to circumstances. In this book they have been taken as 5 years.

Pay-out time   The period in years which is needed to repay the original investment with the aid of the positive cash flow generated by it.

PDV   Abbreviation for present day value.

PEP   Abbreviation for Profitability in the Entire Period. It is defined as the weighted average of the net income as a percentage of the net capital employed during the period which commences when the first capital is spent on the project and terminates $p + q$

years after the plant has gone into operation; p and q can be taken as any number of years according to requirements. They should be equal to those of the corresponding PIP and PAP.

PIP   Abbreviation for Profitability in the Initial Period. It is defined as the weighted average of the net income as a percentage of the net capital employed during the period which commences when the first capital is spent on the project and terminates p years after the project has gone into operation; p can be taken as any number of years according to circumstances. In this book it has been taken as 5 years.

POT   Abbreviation for pay-out time.

Present day value   The aggregate of the present day value of each of the annual cash flows at a given discount rate. Net present value is often used for the same concept.

R Mathematical symbol for any discount rate.

Res. value   Abbreviation for residual value.

Residual value   The aggregate of any amounts (for, e.g., land or working capital) which have to be added back to the cash flow at the end of the life time of the project in order to make the cash flow over the life time of the project balance with the net income over the same period.

S Mathematical symbol for the earning power of any cash flow.

t/a   Abbreviation for tons per annum.

W Mathematical symbol for working capital (cumulative total).

$W_1, W_2, \ldots, W_m$ Mathematical symbols for increases in working capital in years $1, 2, \ldots, m$.

INDEX

influence of a new investment on the profitability of the company   116, 118
- significance of the proportion between fixed investment and working capital on earning power   65–71

Netback
- definition   1, 199

Net capital employed
- definition   11, 201
- computation   11

Net income
- definition   10
- and cash flow   58–61
- time profile   63, 64

NI/NCE
- of the company and growth   118–122
- of the company, and its relationship to earning power, the PIP, PAP and PEP and the growth rate   146–152

Optimisation
- of earning power   95–107
- of PDV   95–107
- of earning power (or PDV) and cost of the product   104

PAIL
- a case study   137–141
- description   138
- and investments "beyond the pale"   139

Pay-out time   201

PIP
- and its desirable relationship to the PAP 132, 133, 135